JOHN HOWE
forging dragons

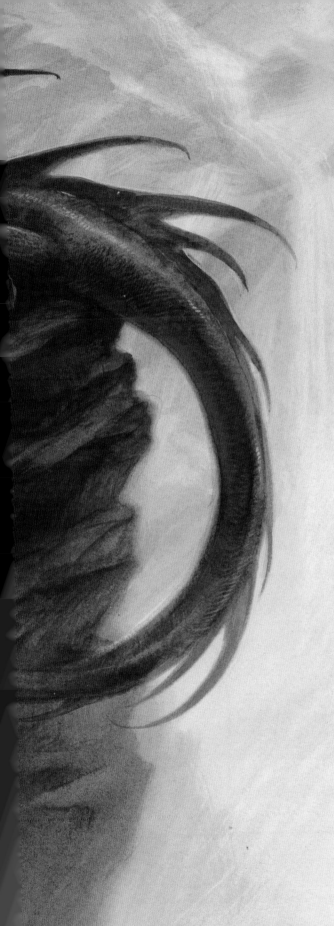

JOHN HOWE

forging dragons

Wing and talon, scale and fire

Might and poison, guile and ire

Traveller, tarry not, hasten far

For this is where the dragons are.

J. Frank-Lynne, WHERE THE DRAGONS ARE

IMPACT

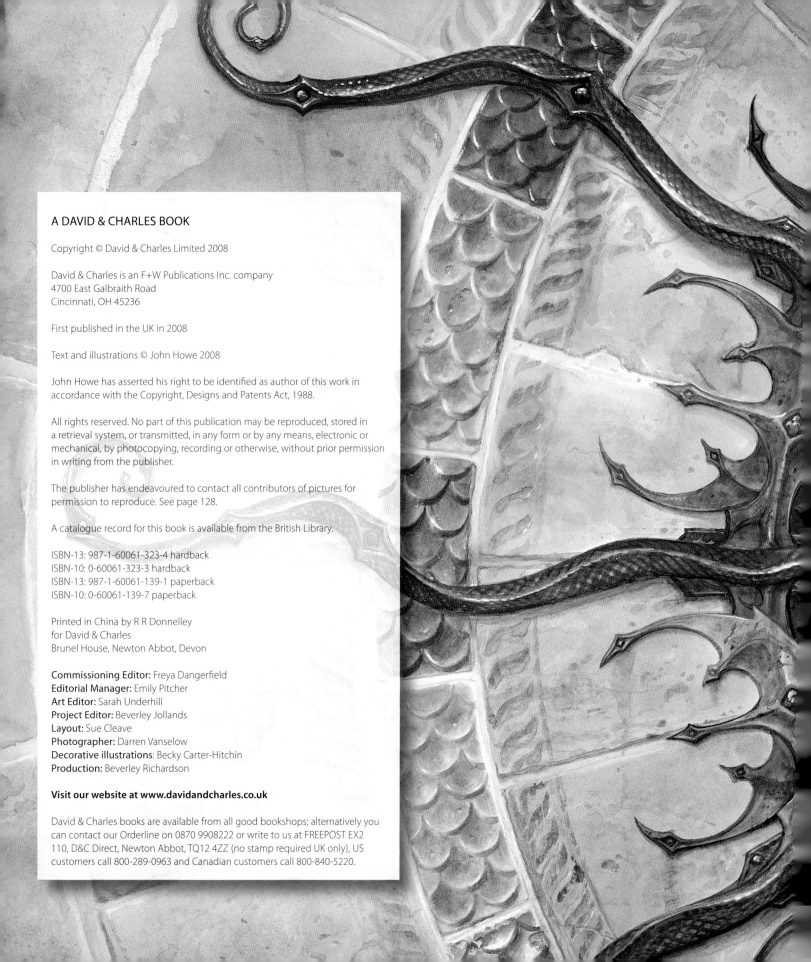

A DAVID & CHARLES BOOK

Copyright © David & Charles Limited 2008

David & Charles is an F+W Publications Inc. company
4700 East Galbraith Road
Cincinnati, OH 45236

First published in the UK in 2008

Text and illustrations © John Howe 2008

ISBN-13: 987-1-60061-323-4 hardback
ISBN-10: 0-60061-323-3 hardback
ISBN-13: 987-1-60061-139-1 paperback
ISBN-10: 0-60061-139-7 paperback

Printed in China by R R Donnelley
for David & Charles
Brunel House, Newton Abbot, Devon

Commissioning Editor: Freya Dangerfield
Editorial Manager: Emily Pitcher
Art Editor: Sarah Underhill
Project Editor: Beverley Jollands
Layout: Sue Cleave
Photographer: Darren Vanselow
Decorative illustrations: Becky Carter-Hitchin
Production: Beverley Richardson

Visit our website at www.davidandcharles.co.uk

David & Charles books are available from all good bookshops; alternatively you
can contact our Orderline on 0870 9908222 or write to us at FREEPOST EX2
110, D&C Direct, Newton Abbot, TQ12 4ZZ (no stamp required UK only), US
customers call 800-289-0963 and Canadian customers call 800-840-5220.

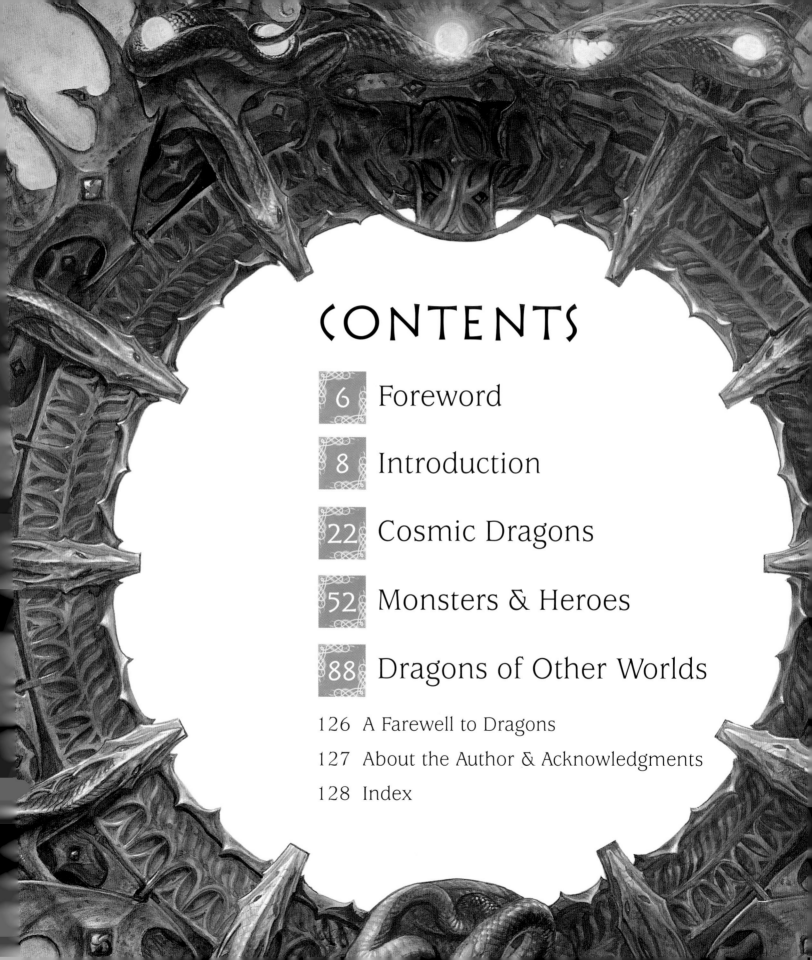

CONTENTS

6 Foreword

8 Introduction

22 Cosmic Dragons

52 Monsters & Heroes

88 Dragons of Other Worlds

126 A Farewell to Dragons

127 About the Author & Acknowledgments

128 Index

FOREWORD BY GUILLERMO DEL TORO

"SVNT DRACONES"

In the original draft of *Pan's Labyrinth* – and all the way into production – the centerpiece of the fairy tale told by Ophelia (the film's main character) to her unborn brother was a striking image: a black, horned dragon, fused with a flint stone mountain, surrounded with thorns. And, at the peak of the mountain, a delicate blue rose that concedes immortality to whomever would dare pluck it.

But so fierce was the dragon (whom I called Varanium Silex) that men preferred to avoid pain than to gain eternal life. The fable was pertinent to the very core of the film's message but, instrumental as it was, the dragon had to be dropped out of the sequence. Money, resources and lack of time conspired to seal that fate...

To this day I miss it so – because, like the rose, the dragon is a polyvalent symbol. One that changes according to each mythology but that retains its universal power. An archetype of sorts. In the book that you now hold in your hands, you will be carefully guided by a studious and engaging guide through a jaw-dropping array of dragons inhabiting the mind of a single man and of all of mankind.

We must consider the singular virtue of the dragon and its position as one of the very few creatures common in nearly all bestiaries around the world. There has been much speculation that perhaps the birth of the dragon in mythology was spurred by an ancestral encounter with large reptilian remains or even the residual memory of the primordial animal in all of us. A composite of every predator of yore – fear and awe inscribed in our very genes. Dragon and man tangled in the dreams of an unending spiral of Xs and Ys.

But I prefer to think that perhaps there is a plane, physical or not, on which dragons do exist. Cartographers of the old world used to mark the forbidden regions, the Finisterre, with daunting beasts that both guarded and populated that which is beyond our grasp. 'Here be Dragons' they would warn, as the map became a Pascalian void. And in examining an old *Mappa Mundi* in my parents' library, I would dream exclusively of exploring that very region.

Whether they hold a pearl, as in their eastern depiction, or they guard a treasure, embedding their chests with jewels and gold – much like Smaug the Magnificent and many before him – dragons have become instrumental in our attempts at understanding the universe within and around us.

Ryu in Japan, Long in China, Naga in Sanskrit. A dragon can symbolize greed or wisdom or prosperity or it can be found swallowing the sun, writhing in the storm or embodying the Fallen One in Christian cosmology, but it will always cast its long shadow upon the walls of our cavern – a primal form in the intelligible world.

The dragon can be the worm and crawl on the earth or soar through the air. Within its massive, noble chest, it holds the essence of the Sun and the power of destruction. Its features have influenced astrology, astronomy, chemistry, botanical nomenclature and, indeed, nearly every venue of human endeavour. Its name has graced the lineage of the ancient kings, from Uther to Arthur and it has been slain by Beowulf, St. George and their infinite permutations. But it has also been tamed by the Buddah and by the cloak of St. Marcel du Paris. For the dragon is equally feared and admired, cherished and longed for as a lost creature of Eden.

Back in 1964, the dragon became my patron at birth – according to the Chinese horoscope – but I would have felt a kinship regardless, because the dragon is the patron saint of all storytellers and artists, and his likeness has adorned canvases and stone and has been forged in every precious metal. It has been emblazoned, embroidered and immortalized by the likes of Leonardo, Uccello, Moreau, Delacroix and now Howe amongst a legion of acolytes.

It is Chinese mythology which reveals that, as a shape-shifter, the dragon can adopt human guise and even procreate with our species, to suffuse us with its fire. And I therefore believe that within each of us sleeps a dragon, waiting to gain significance through our own, everyday acts. It allows us to channel it like an ancestral demiurge to make sense of our place in the cosmos. Or to battle it and conquer all that is unknown to us, giving us all our slice of Finisterre, becoming the key to that which lies beyond.

I have admired John Howe's art for many years; his enviable eye for composition and drama and an almost unerring sense of light. His qualities lie well beyond the technical prowess of a draughtsman. John has a personal universe, a language all of his own. For years, I sought his work gracing books or games but, since then, as a fan, I have welcomed every compilation or book he's ever put out. His holistic view of colour, tone, architectural and textural detail result in unrivaled pieces of storytelling. He doesn't illustrate the tale; he embodies it. On average, a John Howe image is worth 100,000 words. Give or take a couple.

So jump into these erudite, fascinating pages and peek within at some of the most vivid depictions of this beast that belongs to us all. Blessedly, you will find here the ancient cartographers follies, embodied beyond their wildest dreams. 'Here be Dragons' indeed.

Praised be John Howe and may the fire within him never be extinguished.

GUILLERMO DEL TORO
LONDON, 2008

VARANIUM SILEX coils his black length around a mountain top crowned by thorns. On his forehead gleams immortality, within the petals of a pale blue rose.

Dragons are often the embodiment of the worst fears that must be conquered on a quest. Facing them means challenging the dark, confronting most reluctantly that part of ourselves we prefer not to face. From Theseus to Saint George, from Beowulf to Bilbo, all down the long long list of knights and saints and heroes (even the most unlikely or reluctant ones), there always seems to be a dragon in wait.

NTRODUCTION

THIS IS A BOOK ABOUT DRAGONS

ACTUALLY, IT'S SEVERAL BOOKS ...

FIRST, it is an encyclopaedia, since dragons sprawl atop a wealth of lore that equals only their golden treasure troves. Our collective culture is an edifice built brick by brick over millennia by millions of bricklayers, and dragons poke their scaly noses out of every crack and cranny of it; they are ever in the dark space under the stairs, or flying over at great height, wings glinting in the sun, or guarding some door or gate with sharp talon or sly advice. Dragons are so much a part of our subconscious that we rarely consider them carefully (as they are such an intimate part of us, perhaps they don't always invite scrutiny). The book is not, however, an attempt to link dragons to dinosaurs, to root the origins of the great wyrms in some imperceptible and hypothetical recollection from our proto-human past. Nor is it pseudo-science: I am not a fan of cross-sections of dragon plumbing and fire-breathing apparatuses, which erase the magic while providing a wholly unsatisfactory fiction in exchange.

It is, though, a gallery of images, a glossary of scales, a lexicon of tails and talons, a thesaurus of Sauria, a visual exploration of genus *Draköni*. Visually, dragons are a universe to themselves. They present illustrative challenges that involve a curious and simultaneous suspension and reinforcing of belief – they can't exist, but they need to look real, dragging their bellies on the ground, spitting forth great gouts of flame, spreading their wings and taking flight. Quite honestly, I didn't realize I had drawn so many of them, that they had found their way into so many images. But then, they can be devious creatures, despite their size.

SECOND, it is a practical art book: as much as I dislike the term, it does contain a lot of information about how I work, what can go wrong or right in a picture (wrong always makes for better storytelling) and other hints and tips that are the product of much paper covered in colour, as well as signposting the pitfalls of discouragement that punctuate any picture. It is also a guide to treading the path between client and creative conscience. There will be a lot to read between the lines and, added to that, each picture is always worth its weight in words.

THIRD, and perhaps most important, it is, in the form of a book, a representation of the way I work: a combination of encyclopaedic but fully empirical knowledge, both extensive and flawed, rigorous and biased; a desire to see clearly even things that do not exist; an interest in humankind and our visual terms of engagement with the world around us and the worlds in our heads. On the road between all these things, these contradictions and convictions, is where the illustrator of fantasy wanders, sometimes aimlessly, sometimes with a strange sense of urgency and purpose. The book explores the notion of vulnerability to imagery – just how much of what you consider your own personal vision is really yours, and how much is inherited or absorbed. How to deal with the uses of the enchantments involved – what is the part of the subconscious that must enter into your palette, and how to make sure you don't simply ruin it by too much thought – an exercise in studious intuition. How to let your pencil wander and how to follow where it leads. All very romantic, but simultaneously, it is also a hard-nosed exposé of how to draw the things and how to make them crawl and fly. (It's also a nice opportunity to see if all these thoughts that tumble in the happy chaos of my mind can actually be given voices that make sense.) It is an attempt to pin down, even briefly, the infinitely tricky business of why one sees things the way one does, not to make the actual vision valid for others, but in the hope that the method in the madness thus outlined may serve as an example for the reader's personal foray into those lands beyond.

And dragons are the perfect companions for such a voyage, because we all know what they are. Or do we?

WATER, AIR, EARTH AND FIRE A dragon done for a fantasy novel, in which creatures metamorphose through the elements, becoming stone, tree, dolphin and eagle until they assume their final form as dragons. (The most fun I had was developing the esoteric lettering, so esoteric in fact that I've forgotten exactly what it says.)

OCTOBER 2008

SCALES, TALONS, WINGS AND FIRE

I nhabiting the elements of earth, fire, air and water in regions beyond human reach, dragons are crystallizations of natural forces – storms, earthquakes and volcanoes. Tales of godlike heroes vanquishing dragons that threaten the world represent a universal wish to preserve order and safeguard humanity. The dragons and serpents of the ancient creation myths were emblems of chaos; later they came to symbolize not just disorder but evil.

The basic concept of the dragon is familiar all over the world, but there are infinite variations. Dragons may or may not have legs or wings, guard treasure or breathe fire; they may be large enough to encircle the earth or as small as a cat (or both at once). Invariably they are reptilian, hatched from eggs, with scaly bodies, sometimes with dorsal spines and a barbed tail. If they have wings these are usually bat-like and leathery. Some have no legs, some two, four or more.

The word 'dragon' comes from the Greek for a serpent, *drakon*, which is related to *derkesthai*, 'to see', and the dragon's eyes are those of a snake: without eyelids, it has a steady, unblinking gaze. Dragon traditions are rooted in the cosmic serpents of creation mythology and the serpent deities worshipped by ancient cultures. Snake deities usually controlled the rain, and the association with water persists in numerous legends about dragons haunting lakes, wells and springs.

In the western world the suppression of the ancient serpent cults encouraged the view of dragons as hostile or downright evil, but eastern cultures, while still fearing them as unpredictable and potentially destructive, have always honoured them as forces of nature. The nagas of India are semi-divine serpents that guard the earth's treasures and whose yawns cause earthquakes. They are descended from Ananta, the nine-headed cobra, a manifestation of Vishnu the creator. In the Hindu creation myth the gods used the primeval naga Vasuki as a rope to churn the cosmic ocean. Now he lies coiled under the mythical Mount Meru and at the end of the present age will consume the world with his fiery breath.

The myth of the nagas travelled to China and Southeast Asia as Buddhism spread from India. In the Chinese tradition, the dragon comes first in the hierarchy of 360 scaly creatures. It is associated with the east, with sunrise, spring and fertility, and its powers include invisibility and the ability to make itself as small as a silkworm or large enough to fill the space between earth and heaven. It represents the male, yang, principle, while another fabulous creature, the phoenix, represents the female, yin. Together they symbolize marital harmony. Four dragon kings rule the heavens, the oceans and the cardinal points. They bring rain in return for offerings (they are particularly fond of swallows' flesh), but if angered they cause storms, fog, floods and earthquakes. Spending the winter underground, they are traditionally welcomed back with processions as the spring rains arrive and crops can be planted. The dragon kings protect ferrymen and water carriers, and punish those who waste water.

THE IMPERIAL DRAGON

In traditional Chinese iconography, only the imperial dragon is allowed five claws on each foot. Four claws signify the rank of prince, and a court official would have only three. Dragons are often shown playing with a flaming ball or pearl, said to be a symbol of thunder – it is this game that produces rain.

RUSTEM AND THE DRAGON
A malign dragon is one of the perils
encountered by the legendary Persian warrior
Rustem on his journey through the desert. He kills
it with the help of his horse, Raksh.

INSPIRATIONS 1: THE DRAWER MARKED DRAGONS

 have a fairly respectable collection of reference images which occupy drawers that fill a healthy portion of one wall of the studio. I experimented briefly with binders and gave them up as too fastidious to maintain and search through. The themes I visit most often dictate the names on each … one of the deeper drawers is labelled WYRMS.

PILE-UPS
Drawers pile up around my feet as I work on any given image. Photos spill out and collect in drifts and piles.

FAR RIGHT:
RETURN TO SMAUG
Detailing Smaug's head. The clear patches (bands of moonlight from some hole in the cavern roof) and the smoke from his nostrils were done with a kneadable eraser.

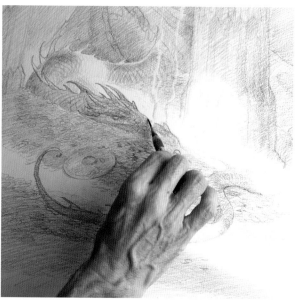

I have numerous books on reptiles, which I constantly use as a reference – not for the actual structure of dragons, but for all the countless details that help to add verisimilitude to their scaly silhouettes. All of these details are used with great indiscrimination; I am not a fan of dragons that owe too many debts to real lizards or dinosaurs, especially in their bodily structures. Nor am I a fan (at all, in fact) of pseudo-scientific attempts at cryptozoology and related disciplines that result in cross-sections of the central-heating and plumbing of dragons, cancelling out their magic and doing nothing else. To me dragons have an overriding 'dragon-ness' that precludes identifying them with earthly animals, be they past or present.

So why is so much documentation required to draw things that don't exist? Wouldn't it be better to let one's imagination wander unencumbered? That would be like asking authors to refrain from reading books. Inspiration requires nurturing, not deprivation. It also requires a minimum of discipline not to simply rely on the haphazardness of images at hand when sketching out ideas, but *looking*, intently and relentlessly, at the world around you. Gathering up reminders of what you've seen will give you a duplicate wealth of worlds: one in your mind where inspiration happens, and one in your image library, so that it is there when you act on that inspiration. (They are complementary, and will only conflict if you delegate the wrong tasks to each. If your search for ideas is done by pawing through a drawer of photos, then you're on as wrong a track as if you ignore your documentation when working on your final piece.)

More often than not I will diligently drag out huge sheaves of documents and arrange them all around my desk, ultimately to ignore most of them. Given that it seems so much easier to take pictures out of drawers than put them back in, diverse and varying strata of themes will accumulate before I can sum up the courage to put them all away again.

Naturally, all this is personal, and is only valid when a degree of realism is sought. A certain fealty is required, both to fantasy and to reality, in order that both contribute to something that is truly unique: your particular world of the imagination.

OPPOSITE: TAKING A STAND ON DRAWING
One of the best contraptions I've ever contrived is my drawing 'pulpit'. It's built at a height to allow comfortable sketching while standing up and, despite coming as an afterthought to a set of built-in bookshelves, it has proved to be indispensable. While it's no full-sized draughtsman's table, it takes up surprisingly little room. (Perhaps I should patent this thing.)

INSPIRATIONS 2: DRAGONS, DRAGONS EVERYWHERE

I have often dreamed of doing a guidebook to Europe following an itinerary that would focus on dragons (the key word here is 'dreamed', but failing that, I do manage to add quite a few to my personal collection in passing). Dragons are popular, so they do tend to end up in the most unexpected places, sudden excerpts in stone or metal from myth and legend, or simply architectural motifs chosen for the aesthetic opportunities they offer.

I find them all fascinating for the glimpses they provide, first into the ingenuity of the sculptors, metalworkers, foundries and artists who created them, then into the history they represent, since they are all themes from another time visited by artists who are, to us, already remote, and finally just because we can walk around them, see them in early morning (before the other tourists) or wait until the light is right (to get a decent view of a particular detail), and in this way, make them fully part of the foundations on which we can build our own imagination. Moreover, unlike the conceit that is illustration (making believe that make-believe is real), these things, for all their imperfections and affiliation with this style or that, are for real, and they offer a healthy dose of the concrete to our hazy musings.

And they are indeed everywhere, from the heady kitsch of the gardens of Versailles to the very Scandinavian wyrms peeking out from the lintels of Kilpeck, from the balconies of Notre-Dame to the mosaics and ironwork of Gaudí's Barcelona.

Saints George and Michael dutifully and tirelessly behead, stab and trample them by the thousand, they have found 'formes varyous' under the hammers of generations of blacksmiths, and they spit veritable rivers of water from eaves everywhere, through throats of copper and sandstone. They lend their shapes to aquamaniles, leer from Viking carvings in museums, coil up the façades of cathedrals and *stavkirkene* (when they aren't lurking in some crypt) and obligingly hold lamps suspended from their iron jaws. They seem to be everywhere, if you take the trouble to look.

Here be dragons indeed.

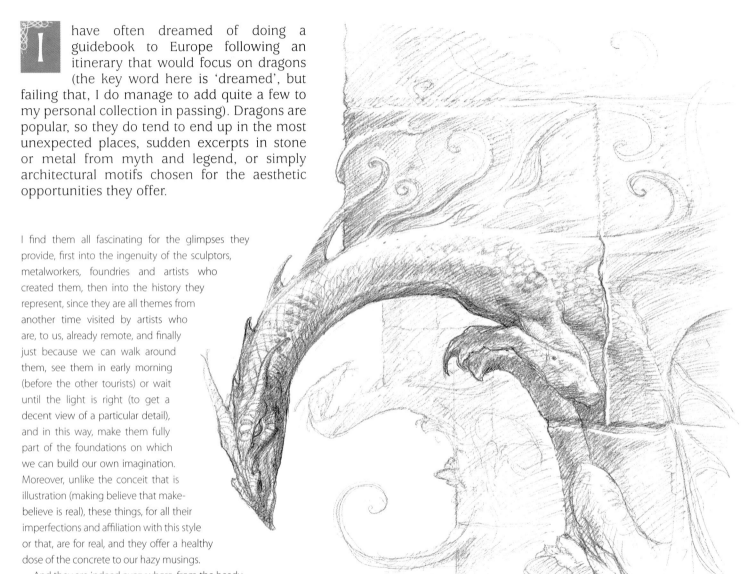

STONEWYRMS

If I had a cathedral to build, this is the kind of detail it would have. (Alas, I was born nearly a thousand years too late.) To be able to build real fantasy designs in actual stone would simply be a dream come true. Our house, though, does have a rainspout in the shape of a dragon. It's a start.

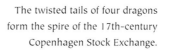

Winged dragon holding a lantern
in a Venice street.

The twisted tails of four dragons
form the spire of the 17th-century
Copenhagen Stock Exchange.

The Dragon Fountain
in the garden of the
Palace of Versailles.

Art Nouveau
St George and dragon
by Eusebi Arnau,
Casa Amatller,
Barcelona.

Winged dragon supporting a balcony
in Bredgade, Copenhagen.

Grotesque looking down on
Paris from between the towers of
Notre-Dame.

Baby iron dragon clinging to a grille
on Gaudi's Casa Vicens, Barcelona.

Ouroboros on the south door of
the 12th-century Kilpeck Church,
Herefordshire.

François Bosio's Hercules
killing the Lernaean Hydra,
Tuileries, Paris.

omposition is something I never really think about. It's so entwined in narrative that I can't consider one without the other: it's driven by the picture's internal space and the acknowledgement of that space (or not) by the protagonists, as well as by the nature of the piece. But, if obliged to think about it …

If the image is a hieratic, or iconic, one, the composition is drawn in on itself to centre things, rather than having the narrative carry it outside the borders of the picture. This kind of 'poster image' is essentially a composition in two dimensions. The scene relies on our unique viewpoint for the positioning of the elements: the

relationship between them, whether animate or inanimate, is for the viewer's benefit, not theirs.

Conversely, a narrative image relies on the imagined 'stage' for the placing of the characters and other elements. They take up their spots in the scene in relation to each other and the action – not the viewer. Naturally there is an overlay of compositional considerations, but it does not drive the layout. Its importance is dependant on the 'distance' from the narrative: comics and graphic novels are the most immediate, plunging the viewer into the midst of the action, with extravagant foreshortenings and perspectives, recreating a blow-by-blow narrative, coming closer to cinema than illustration. Traditional illustration draws back slightly, at least outside (or beside) the action, to a slightly more comfortable viewing spot.

Adhering to compositional rules involving golden numbers, means and sections means sacrificing narrative devices in favour of a language of symbolism and allegory. Something like a stage, where the wings do not exist except to allow actors to enter from the limbo that is offstage. (Nothing happens offstage, it only really happens when it is *recounted* onstage.) Ignoring strict rules of composition means that the narrative will instinctively impose the framing of a portion of the explicit action, while the implicit action (what's gone before, what's coming next or what's happening right now but offstage) is understood more by intuition than cogitation.

The more anecdote the less symbolism is perhaps a good rule. Pure visual anecdote doesn't leave much room for extra baggage. Purely symbolic imagery retains anecdote only to the extent that it remains figurative: all other content relies on a sharing of cultural significance. I regret not being able to walk into a cathedral and read the mosaics, frescos and statuary as a medieval person would. (Doubtless I could do some serious homework, and acquire the knowledge to do it, but the spiritual meaning would still escape me.)

In the sketch of St Michael on page 73, the composition is all golden sections and squared spaces and bisected circles; in the one of Sigurd and Fafnir on page 69, the narrative is all waiting to happen, poised in that split second before he stabs the dragon. But all that happens of its own accord, because it's subordinate to the material and the understanding of and approach to that material. That's the reason, I suppose, why I am forced to admit I never really think about it, or only when obliged.

RED NAILS SKETCH
This sketch was done on several layers of tracing paper. First, I drew Conan to make sure that his proportions were right, and then coiled the serpent all about him, from the top down, like a garland around a Christmas tree.

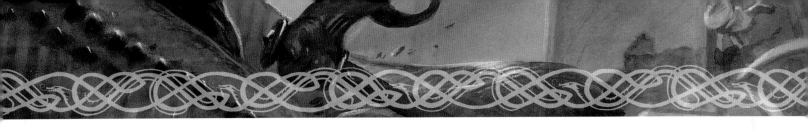

RED NAILS ARTWORK

The actual logisitics of the painting involved quite a lot of airbrush, especially for the shadows.

The focal point of the whole thrashing creature is here, at the top of the triangle formed by Conan's stance.

Curves are never directionless, they are always going somewhere and doing something on their way. Not to take advantage of their inherent tetradimensionality would be a shame. (I'm not beyond inventing the occasional neologism; this one of course means three dimensions with the notion of time – and thus movement – attached.)

Details like this are mainly for fun, but also to reinforce the stop-action side of the picture.

DRAGON FEATURES
AND VARIATIONS

There are dragons that resemble snakes, crocodiles, lizards, even dogs and horses. There are dragons with three, seven or a hundred heads, and some with a head at each end. Dragons, in all their shapes and sizes, have bred and prospered through the retelling of stories and legends, the astonishing descriptions of returning travellers and the inventiveness of medieval heralds and compilers of bestiaries.

The largest and oldest tend to be serpents and sea monsters. Without wings or legs, they are sometimes described as wyrms (or worms) – a term also used in a derogatory way of dragons generally. Such beasts may lie coiled around hills or mountains, or even coiled around the world itself. The cosmic wyrm Ouroboros, which holds its tail in its mouth, has a smaller relative called the amphisbaena, which wears a second head on its tail and can roll itself into a hoop to chase its prey. One head keeps watch while the other sleeps. The multi-headed dragons of Slavic folklore are the descendants of monsters of antiquity, such as the Hydra and the beast of the Apocalypse. Of the Hydra's many heads only one was immortal, but as each was cut off two would grow in its place. Heracles solved this problem by cauterizing each stump with a firebrand and burying the immortal head under a rock.

ABOVE: DRAKHAOUL

A sketch for a book cover. The hero is inhabited by the spirit of a daemon, the Drakhaoul, who must drink blood to maintain his physical form – that of a powerful winged dragon. The author's invention draws deeply on Eastern European lore, which makes this kind of exercise all the more fun. The line down the middle of the drawing is the gutter of my sketchbook. Even an A3 sketchbook can be far too small.

OPPOSITE: ELVES AND DRAGONS

A follow-up sketch on the theme of a race of Elves who ride vast dragons. This dragon is missing a wing, in order to see their structure properly. The actual wing itself filled up another entire sheet of paper. Dragons' wings are rarely drawn big enough.

Babylonian dragons resemble winged hounds or lions, but most dragons are built on lizard lines, with four legs, though some have only two and others more. Heraldic artists defined the appearance of subspecies such as the wyvern (with two legs, two wings and a barbed tail), the lindworm (a wingless wyvern) and the cockatrice, a winged lizard with the head of a rooster. Some individual dragons had unique attributes. The fire-breathing Tarasque of Provence was armoured like a turtle, with six bear-like legs, a scorpion's tail, a lion's mane and the face of a sad old man; another French monster, the Peluda, had a snake's head and tail, turtle's feet and a body covered in shaggy green hair or, according to another account, stinging porcupine quills that it could fire at its enemies.

DRAWING FROM LIFE:
FANTASY AND REALITY

I think dragon life-drawing courses should be mandatory in art schools. The whole idea of lending a sense of reality to fantasy is based on an avid assimilation of detail and surface with a suppleness of approach and a certain freedom when it comes to structure.

I confess to relying heavily on photos for detail, but never for the initial sketch. It's far better to have a certain understanding of animal anatomy and not get bogged down too early in speculative structural considerations. Putting life into fantasy means not tampering with the fantastical nature of beings, but building up realistic details where they are meaningful. Copy-pasting a heterogeneous collection of details is not the answer. Reinforcing your vision of any fantastical creature through the indirect process of freely sketching what your mind's eye sees is a far more personal and satisfying method than building up a universe by sewing a surrealist patchwork of details.

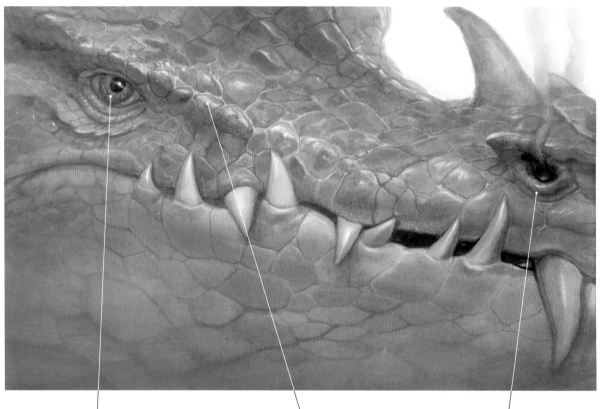

THE BLUE DRAGON
The original was done to be printed in one colour for a book's endpapers, but not taking advantage of the contrasts and colours would have been a shame, so I ended up doing it in full colour – a decsion that turned out to be very wise.

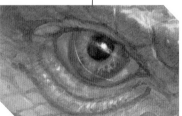

Reptile's eyes are far more interesting than ours, with nictating membranes, slit pupils and other exciting features. In this case I did a vaguely human eye – a little anthropomorphism doesn't always hurt.

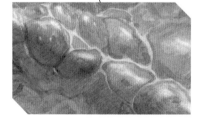

Crocodile skin. Working here from close-up photos and concentrating on getting those little spaces between scales right, as well as working up the volume of each scale.

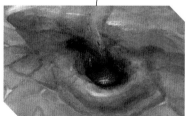

Where there's smoke ... the fire in nostril and mouth was done by scraping off the grey-blue and adding vermillion and sparks. The smoke is coloured pencil.

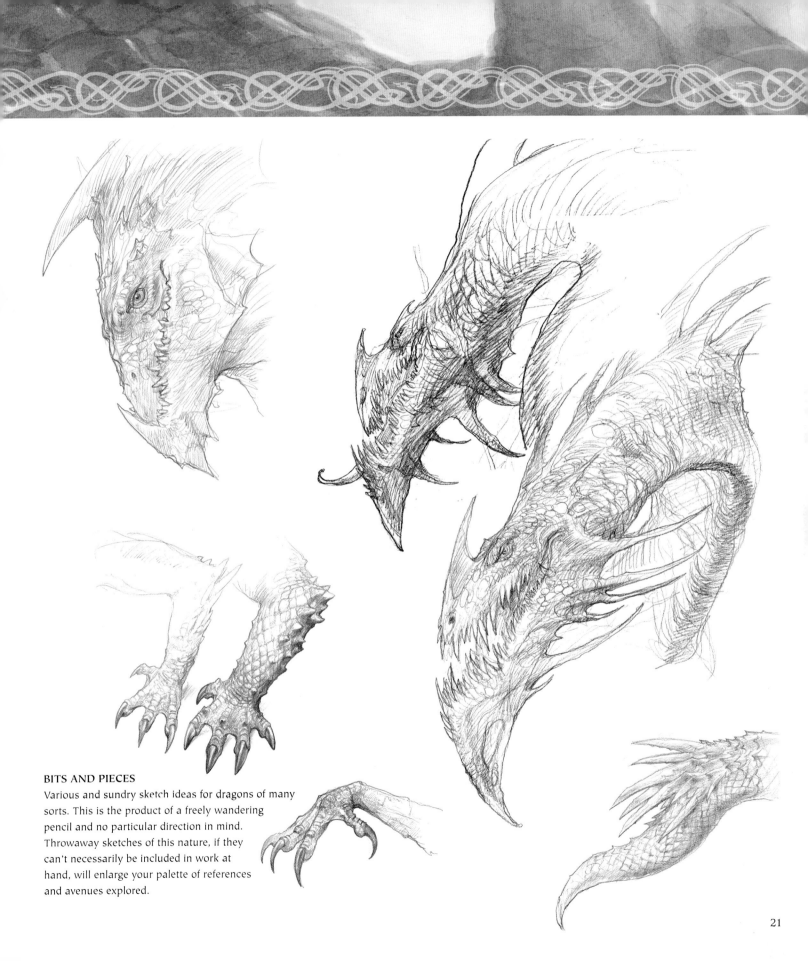

BITS AND PIECES

Various and sundry sketch ideas for dragons of many sorts. This is the product of a freely wandering pencil and no particular direction in mind. Throwaway sketches of this nature, if they can't necessarily be included in work at hand, will enlarge your palette of references and avenues explored.

21

COSMIC DRAGONS

Born out of the mists and swirling waters that existed before the beginning of time, dragons and serpents writhe and glide through humanity's earliest stories. They are central to creation myths around the world, encircling the earth or lurking in the lowest regions of the universe. Their size is infinite and their form unknown, yet the dragon is a powerful symbol in every culture.

TIAMAT

How to depict something that by definition has no form? In Sumerian and Babylonian mythology the body of the great dragon Tiamat exists before creation, because she is the material from which the universe will be made. She is the primordial salt-water ocean, the embodiment of chaos, and her consort is the fresh-water ocean, Apsu – the mingling of the two engenders the gods and the world emerges from the subsequent battles between these parents and their turbulent offspring.

THE GOD AND THE DRAGON

Ancient renderings of mythological events are often not of great practical use for modern illustrators, but I do try always to familiarize myself with related imagery. This is an impression of a neo-Assyrian cylinder seal from 900–750 BC: a horned reptile with two legs, perhaps Tiamat, is being attacked by a bearded god, holding a six-pronged thunderbolt and arrows, and a smaller god with a spear, while a goddess opens her arms to grab the creature's snout.

The Babylonian epic of creation describes Tiamat as a female dragon, with immense horns, a serpentine body and two forelegs. Apsu, growing tired of the gods he has fathered, plots to destroy them. Tiamat refuses to take part, but when Ea the water god captures Apsu and Mummu (the waves), Tiamat spawns an army of monsters and attacks Ea and the other gods. (Isn't this just fabulous stuff? Not easy to put into any form of figurative or narrative image, but so rich in possibilities it makes one's head swim.) The gods persuade Marduk, Ea's son, to challenge her in battle by offering him all their powers, making him supreme. Armed with this power, and with the prospect of becoming the god of gods, Marduk dons his armour, gathers up his weapons and sets forth against his mother.

Marduk slays the army of monsters. As Tiamat goes to swallow him, he throws a storm into her open mouth so that she can't close her jaws, then catches her in a net. He splits her skull and slashes her body in half: one half forms the ocean floor and the other the heavens. He pierces her eyes, which become the sources of the rivers

Tigris and Euphrates, and curls her immense tail in the sky to form the Milky Way. Having thus created the world, Marduk then sets about populating it by killing Tiamat's son Kingu, and mixing his blood with earth to create humankind.

The sheer scale of creation myths, from the most ancient, like this one, to the versions inserted in folktale as anecdote, is really staggering. Nevertheless, we humans are placed right in the middle of them through our identification with the gods, who will ultimately tame chaos to create the world. This curious mix of anecdote and dimensionless, timeless space is fascinating to try to depict.

Creating order from chaos

In many traditions the story starts with water: the turbulent, churning ocean, the emblem of primeval chaos on to which light breaks. The watery abyss is stirred up by a fiery, bright, new arrival – a god of light – who sets the process in motion and produces an orderly universe from the formless, timeless confusion of the primeval soup.

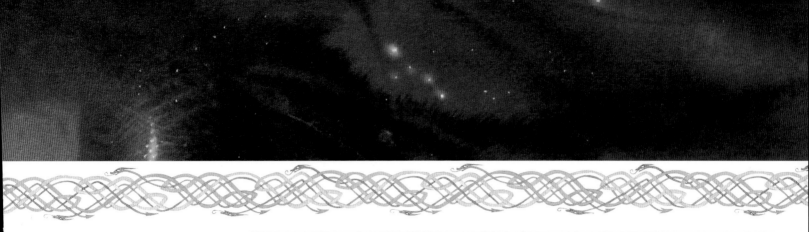

THE BIRTH OF STARS

Telescopes like Hubble provide imagery that is practically mythological already: perfect for creations of universes. This is star cluster NGC346, about 210,000 light years away in the dynamic star nursery known as the Small Megellanic Cloud, a satellite galaxy of the Milky Way.

Equally common is the figure who appears in opposition to the bright spirit of the creator as the embodiment of the old chaos: this is the dragon or serpent, the child of darkness, wyrm of evil intent, hater of light. In the Sumerian story that appears to be the source for Tiamat, the monster is Kur, the personification of the underworld, referred to as 'the monster who holds back the waters'. (This same description is also used of the cosmic serpent in Indian and South American myths.) Kur is killed by the hero Ninurta, who stems the resulting floods by piling stones on the monster's body – just as many dragons are entombed in later stories to prevent their destructive power from ever breaking free.

PAINTING THE DRAGON

I dug out every book I could find that had photos of distant galaxies, emptied my 'Outer Space' drawer and spread everything all around my page, then sketched in a semblance of a layout: a little circle for Marduk, to remember where he would go and establish a direction for the confrontation, and a few lines to establish the neck, head and bloated body of Tiamat. Then I prepared a plate with puddles of purple and pink, another of blues of several hues and a third of black ink, and basically threw it all over the paper.

**OPPOSITE: SKETCH –
DRAGON OF CHAOS**
I'd be tempted to call this a doodle gone wild ... and aptly so, given the subject. After a while the patchwork juxtaposing of features reached the edge of the paper and stopped, but I would happily start again on the same scale on a sheet ten times as large. The danger, though, comes when you begin to apply method to this wandering of pencil on paper and lose spontaneity. This is one I really want to do in colour.

TIAMAT AND MARDUK
There is really no controlling this kind of exercise with any precision, but those fan-shaped brushes used for smoothing oils are ideal, allowing you to coax colours about without creating hard lines. Keeping the paper damp for as long as possible is crucial. The rest is building on and reacting to spontaneous puddling and bleeding of colours with pretty much every soft brush you own until things begin to settle. As the paper dries you can work on smaller and smaller effects until you run out of damp areas to work in. It's also wise to have a hairdryer handy to prevent the colours drying unevenly, though it can be an interesting feature if it happens in the right place. All the little features that are more or less figurative – the head, wings and scales here and there – were added later with a dry brush, or worked up in coloured pencil. The stars are acrylic, with a touch of airbrushed white gouache to help them shine.

In what is basically
a cosmic conflict
of the generations,
Marduk, the young
god, approaches in a
blaze of light to destroy
his mother Tiamat,
shooting an arrow deep
into her body. He will
create the heavens and
earth from her vast
remains.

APEP, ENEMY OF RE

I n such an immobile and sunbaked country as the Valley of the Nile, it seems only natural that the Ancient Egyptian Underworld should be a particularly dark, doleful and perilous place. This is where the cosmic serpent Apep lurked, waiting to ambush the sun god Re as he voyaged through the darkness each night towards the eastern horizon, from where he would rise again. Apep, who was wholly evil, had existed since before creation and could never be destroyed.

THE OVERTHROWING OF APEP
Re the sun god, in the form of the great cat of Helopolis, kills Apep under the city's sacred Persea tree, in a wall painting from the tomb of Inherkhau at Deir el-Madinah, 20th dynasty.

Images of Re-Herakhty, the falcon-headed god of the rising sun, show him holding the vanquished serpent under his talons. But while Apep was repeatedly defeated, he already inhabited the land of the dead: the following night he would be ready to attack again. He was conceived as a giant snake or serpent, later as a dragon, and was called 'World Encircler', 'Enemy of Re', 'Evil Lizard' or 'Serpent of Rebirth'. Some said he waited just below the western horizon and others that he attacked in the east, just before dawn. He was the most dangerous of Re's enemies, intent on devouring the sun, and would swallow the waters of the celestial river or choke the channel with his coils to strand the solar boat.

For a civilization that valued order above all else, darkness and chaos, as embodied by Apep and his fellow creatures, was the greatest adversary. The battle was enjoined daily, and it would go on forever. Ma'at, the goddess of order, governed the seasons, stars and all the actions of humans and gods from the moment of creation. She maintained truth and justice and guarded against a return to chaos – an ever-present danger in the person of Apep. She shepherded the sun through the sky.

But Apep did win battles. Storms and earthquakes were his victories. He even managed to catch and swallow the sun from time to time, but Re was always quickly freed of the solar eclipse by the defenders who travelled with him. Only the god Set had the power to kill Apep, aided by the serpent Mehen, who threw his coils around Apep while Set speared him. Among Re's other defenders was the scorpion goddess Serqet, who had power over reptiles and poisonous animals and could thus hold Apep's tail. Maahes, the lion god of war, protected Re during his battle, while Shu, the god of the air and wind who held up the sky, used spells to protect the boat.

Of course, killing the ruler of the dead could not be permanent, and Apep would simply reappear when Re's sunboat sank below the horizon. Only the continued prayers and rituals of the people could ensure his nightly defeat. Priests of the New Kingdom

SET DEFENDS RE
Set spears Apep from the solar boat in a vignette from the papyrus Book of the Dead of Lady Cheritwebeshet, 21st dynasty.

RE'S SOLAR BARQUE
A 4th-century BC insignia in the form of a solar barque dedicated to Djedher, used in processions and funerary rites. The boat holds a shrine containing the sun god.

enacted an annual ceremony called the Banishing of Apep. An effigy of the serpent was ritually burnt, in the hopes that all the evil of Egypt would burn with it. The Books of Overthrowing Apep detailed procedures for subduing him: spitting at him, kicking him, slicing him into pieces and burning him. There were instructions for making models or drawings of the monster, to be destroyed while reciting protective spells. Spells for the destruction of Apep were sometimes included in burials, to protect the dead on their way to the underworld. Maintaining order in the face of chaos was a daily task, and a serious business.

To avoid the pictures themselves adding to Apep's power, ancient images almost always show him being stabbed by a deity. Pharaohs of the New Kingdom played a ritual game of bat and ball in which

the ball represented Apep's 'evil eye'. Each time the king hit the ball with a club, standing for the 'eye of Re', he was symbolically driving away the hostile Apep.

Re's solar barque was very much like the papyrus boats that plied the Nile or the ceremonial boats included in burials. At death the pharaoh was transported in the solar boat to join his father, Re, and the sun's nightly voyage through the underworld corresponded with the journey of the dead – each dawn reassured the Egyptians that they, like the sun, would survive their encounter with the terrible serpent.

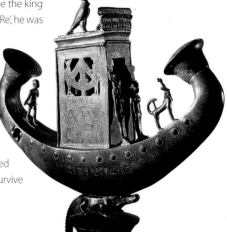

31

SKETCHING THE DRAGON

While I may be a great one for detailing ancient legend and reeling off hard-to-remember names deity by deity, I don't always manage to practise what I preach. I will happily read through tomes and tomes of lore, and then as happily draw what I feel like, regardless. I am convinced, however, that my encyclopaedic reading sinks in on some level and that this gentle and persistent osmosis will eventually enrich the work, without enslaving it to detail conscientiously gleaned and catalogued. Added to that, I find faraway cultures take some drawing to understand – an opportunity that is not always available on a given commission. So, for my brief foray into the Egyptian underworld, I imagined Apep trying one last time to catch Re before the sacred barque rose over the eastern horizon.

APEP SKETCH
An initial sketch gave me an idea of Apep's physiology, a sort of serpent-whale, miles long, twisting and writhing through the water. But in the same project, I had a little too many hump-backed sea creatures cresting the waves, so it was abandoned in favour of this sudden scribble in felt pen jauntily labelled 'Egyptian'.

THE SOLAR BOAT

Painting Re's barque did make me pause a moment; a fine balance is needed between anecdote and myth to ensure that images function both narratively and symbolically. I decided on a simple barque with no crew, with the sun in place of the sail. Sometimes less is more.

At the seventh hour of the night Re faces his most fearful challenge, the serpent-demon Apep. His crew of deities lunge at the creature with their spears; the boat escapes the ravening jaws and sails on towards the dawn, while Apep awaits his next opportunity to attack.

OUROBOROS

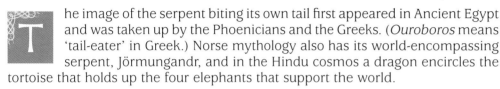

The image of the serpent biting its own tail first appeared in Ancient Egypt and was taken up by the Phoenicians and the Greeks. (*Ouroboros* means 'tail-eater' in Greek.) Norse mythology also has its world-encompassing serpent, Jörmungandr, and in the Hindu cosmos a dragon encircles the tortoise that holds up the four elephants that support the world.

SYMBOL OF UNITY
Alchemists used the ouroboros to represent the unity of matter. This version, inscribed 'All is one', appears in the *Chrysopoea of Cleopatra*, from Alexandrian Egypt.

In ancient cosmologies the earth is surrounded by water, which preserves it by supplying rain, but also threatens flood: the encircling serpent holds back the waters, but can also hold back the rain. In the Rig Veda the monster of drought is defeated by Indra, lord of the storm. His Mayan equivalent, the god Chaac, wields thunderbolts and supplies rain, while the cosmic serpent holds back the waters. The circular image (like the Chinese yin-yang symbol) embraces the notion of the world's existence depending on opposing forces held in balance.

That this personification of the elements, which are eternal in their vast underpinnings, but oft unreliable season to season (rain will fall, inevitably, but will it be in a month or a year – or seven years?) should take the form of a serpent is a gift from ancient times to the fantasy illustrator of today. The rich variety and curious consistency of these legends is not only visually exciting but a very real connection to the curious business of putting images to archaic themes and tales.

The serpent is a creature of the earth, found under stones and roots, in caves and crevices, and associated with death and the underworld. But it also represents renewal and resurrection because of the shedding of its skin in an apparent rebirth. In surrounding the world, the image of the ouroboros implies the existence of something 'outside', and Christians used it to symbolize the limits of the material world, and the self-consuming, transitory nature of mortal existence. Yet its feeding on itself conveys the cycle of existence, an eternal renewal. Jung considered it an archetype, a symbol of universal integration.

I have to suppress quiet yelps of delight when I re-read resumés like this. Consistence and contradiction, constancy and transformation, everything is there. Such an abundance of information means it cannot be dealt with intellectually by image (who wants an encyclopedia in picture form?), it needs to be approached intuitively, armed with a good book on snakes (the practical side) and a familiarity with the World Serpent and his ancestors and offspring (the freedom to imagine). Besides, it's not

likely our ancestors sat down with a list of animals and did a poll to choose which one best represented which concept. The process of image-making inspired by the distant past is as firmly anchored in ancient lives lived long ago as it is in our subconscious today, and it happens in the same places of the mind we go to find – or not – the fantasy imagery we wish to paint. Primitive people would have been 'interested in the subject as such, the object as such, and the relations between them … An original, moving, shapeless or undifferentiated world must be brought to rest and given stable form.'[1] For this reason, I am a great collector of catalogues and diligent visitor of exhibitions and museums. Each trip or book is an opportunity to draw closer to this relation between object and subject, providing the tools to create one's own versions.

Alchemical dragons

For the alchemists, too, the ouroboros was a symbol of integration, the unity of matter in which they tried to discover the seed of gold: the elusive philosopher's stone. In the arcane and allusive style of alchemical texts designed to guard the secrecy of their experiments, they used images of dragons to represent many aspects of the processes of distillation, sublimation and transmutation: the raw material was a green dragon, a winged dragon stood for a volatile element, a wingless dragon for a fixed one. The dragon was generally identified with mercury, known as the father of all metals and vital to the process of transmuting base metal into gold.

Sometimes identified with the philosopher's stone was the marvellous gem, draconite, which had the power to drive out poisons and instil courage and was to be found in the brain of a dragon. It was harder than diamond, but had to be obtained from the still-living beast, as its power ebbed with the dragon's strength.

The imagery of alchemy is a fabulous source for an illustrator, given that perceived truths are always hidden in arcane and esoteric symbolism. I have a good number of books on alchemy (or rather I have a good number of heavily illustrated picture books on alchemy), from which I indiscriminately lift symbols and such when required.

THE ALCHEMISTS' OUROBOROS

There's really nothing very original about the drawing becoming a three-dimensional form and emerging from the page. I confess I'm almost embarrassed to look at this kind of graphic device now, but at the time (the picture dates from the 1990s) I thought I was being quite clever.

The Greek script is copied from a manuscript, and no, I certainly don't know exactly what it says, but I did choose a page that is related to the ouroboros.

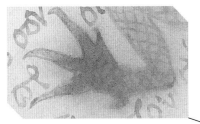

Trying to imitate an archaic draughtsmanship is not always the easiest of undertakings, though it does help to use the same tools – a fine quill pen can guide your hand in a direction you might not normally take with modern instruments.

PAINTING
THE DRAGON

Geometrically, the image of the ouroboros couldn't be simpler: draw circle; fill in wyrm; make sure tail firmly in mouth. Add legs (optional).

Draconologically (or perhaps dragontifically – could the study of dragons be a science?) he is of course much more interesting, as he is the container of chaos, the what's-beyond, the realm outside the lights of the lamps and candles that hold the darkness at bay. But, graphically, he's even more fun. Reconciling the very idea of a world-encompassing wyrm with the task of depicting it can lead down unexpected paths. I haven't really come to terms with how he should or indeed could look, so every time I approach him, it is from a different angle.

COLOUR DETAIL

Getting this kind of effect with water-soluble inks in a good old-fashioned airbrush takes a bit of thought before tackling it. The snake and the satellite view of earth were painted up separately, then masked off. The sky came next, first the blue in ink, then the black in gouache (to allow the overpainting of the planets with their names and orbits), letting the sky go to white around the snake. Third step: painting the red by filling in the white area reserved for it – the tricky bit is overlapping colours while keeping the density equal – and finally a little coat of vermillion to blur the edges of the creature, and a few highlights done with a scalpel and coloured pencil. Vaguely alchemical, in a way, and a huge sense of relief that most of the things that could have gone wrong didn't.

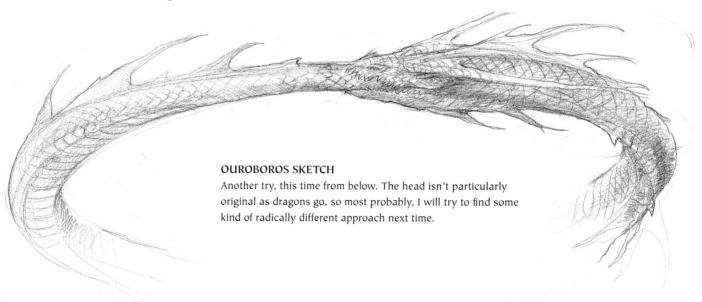

OUROBOROS SKETCH

Another try, this time from below. The head isn't particularly original as dragons go, so most probably, I will try to find some kind of radically different approach next time.

OUROBOROS

This started with a few lines drawn with a compass – one of those sketches where you really have no idea where you're headed. As it turns out, I went in circles, before becoming wholly absorbed and distracted by the idea that I might somehow fit the name – all those Os – inside the wyrm. (I lost interest when I finally managed, after much erasing, to complete the over-and-under Celtic interlace in the letters.)

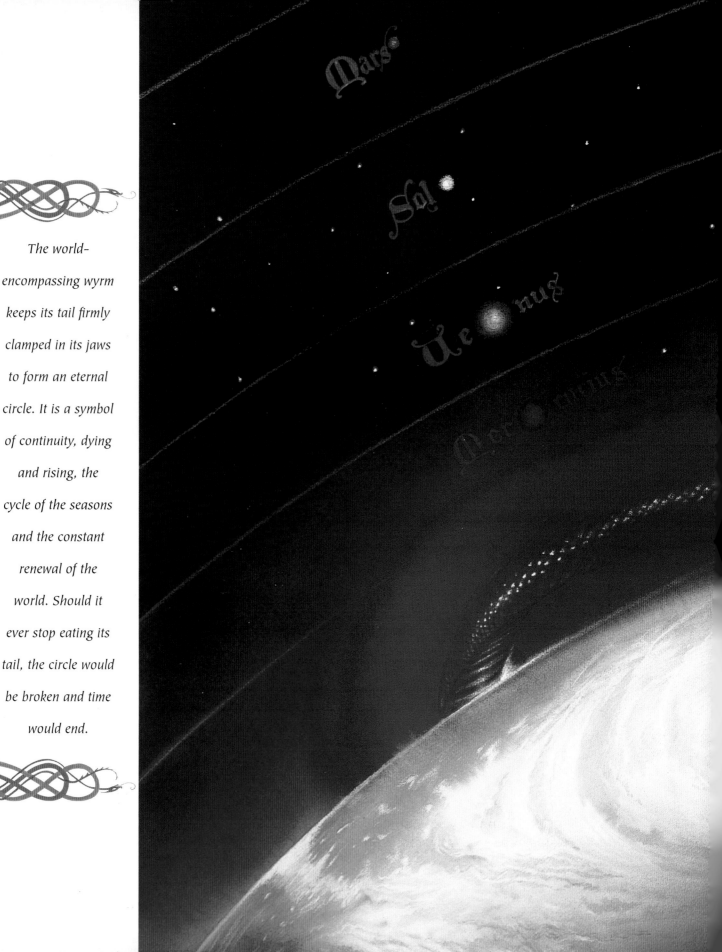

The world-encompassing wyrm keeps its tail firmly clamped in its jaws to form an eternal circle. It is a symbol of continuity, dying and rising, the cycle of the seasons and the constant renewal of the world. Should it ever stop eating its tail, the circle would be broken and time would end.

NIDHOGGR

In the Norse cosmos, the wyrm Nidhoggr bites and tears at the roots of the world tree Yggdrasil, but the tree (and therefore the universe) survives these assaults because it is fed and watered by the three Norns, or Fates: Urd (the past), Verdandi (the present) and Skuld (the future). Nidhoggr, whose name means 'malice striker', is the dragon of death, feeding on the flesh of corpses and drinking their blood.

**THOR'S
FISHING TRIP**
This really needs colour – and perhaps a different perspective – to properly portray just a hint of Jörmungandr in the depths below Hymir's boat.

**VIKING
SERPENT**
Seventh-century Viking brooch in the form of the world serpent.

The World Tree, Yggdrasil, is a great ash, the tree from which the god Odin hung for nine days and nights to learn the wisdom of the runes (Odin's staff is a branch cut from Yggdrasil, in exchange for one of his eyes.), and it grows up through the Norse universe, linking the realms of gods, giants, elves and mortals. The old stories refer to the regions around the tree as the 'nine worlds', though their actual number is uncertain and their locations hazy and shifting.

Yggdrasil's roots extend down into Niflheim, the realm of ice and the domain of Hel. Here lies the serpent-infested wellspring of Hvergelmir, source of all the world's rivers, and here the terrible wyrm Nidhoggr has his lair. High above is Asgard, the realm of the gods. Here stands Odin's hall Valhalla, where the noblest of fallen warriors are brought from the battlefield by the Valkyries to feast and carouse, drinking mead that flows from the udders of the goat Heidrun, who grazes on the leaves of the World Tree.

An eagle sits in the topmost branches, exchanging insults with Nidhoggr via the squirrel Ratatosk, who runs up and down the rotting trunk. Meanwhile the gods ride daily across Bifrost, the rainbow bridge, to reach the Well of Urd where they hold their councils. The Norns sit by the well and use its waters to sustain the tree.

Bifrost links Asgard with Midgard, the world of mortals, which is encircled by another great wyrm, the monstrous Midgard Serpent, Jörmungandr. One of the horrid offspring of the trickster god Loki, he was tossed by Odin into the sea, where he has grown so large that he can surround the world, grasping his tail in his mouth. The sea he swims in separates Midgard from Utgard, the outer world, where the giants of frost and fire have their realms.

Jörmungandr is the arch-enemy of the thunder god Thor, and one of the most popular motifs in Norse pagan art is Thor's fishing trip with the giant Hymir. As the two are on bad terms, Hymir refuses to give Thor any bait, so the god helps himself to the head of Hymir's best ox. They row farther and farther out to sea, catching whales and lions, until Thor finally hooks the poisonous Jörmungandr. He raises his hammer to kill his catch, but the terrified Hymir cuts the line and the serpent gets away.

Thor and the Midgard Serpent are destined to fight to the death at Ragnarok, the battle that will destroy the gods and giants and tear the world apart. On that day, Jörmungandr will slink on to the shore, spewing venom that will poison the earth and sky. The Well of Urd will freeze so that it can no longer nourish Yggdrasil, and Nidhoggr

OPPOSITE: YGGDRASIL AND THE NINE WORLDS
I'm quite uncomfortable doing schematic paintings. It comes much more easily in pencil, so this drawing is a sort of visual shorthand to help me recall the essential portions of the incredibly complicated and occasionally contradictory universe of Norse myth. Of course there is no way to make it all fit in a satisfactory manner.

will finally chew through the roots. The torment of wicked souls will never end, however: in a terrible hall with walls woven from serpents whose venom flows in corrosive streams across the floor, the dragon gnaws in perpetuity on the corpses of murderers, liars and adulterers.

The Norse universe is one the most fascinating, rich and jumbled in mythology, and has not one but *two* huge serpent-wyrms. Most of what we know today was set down by Snorri Sturlusson in the Prose or Younger Edda in the 13th century. With the Poetic or Elder Edda, as well as the Volsungsaga, the Gesta Danorum and Beowulf, it should be part of the essential library of every self-respecting fantasy enthusiast. Honest.

Norse myths not only inspired authors like Tolkien, but they exemplify the 'foreshortening' of reality and myth, in a constant juxtaposing of symbolic motifs and anecdote. Jörmungandr encircles the world, but Thor with his fishing line can nevertheless draw him up to the surface (he pulls so hard that he drives his legs through the boat and plants them on the ocean floor). In another episode, Thor is challenged to lift a cat sleeping on the floor of the giants' hall. Strain as he might, he cannot do it, because the cat is actually Jörmungandr; now just *how* do you illustrate *that*? I've never really made a serious foray into Norse myth, but it is only a question of time.

As for Nidhoggr, I would happily paint and re-paint him until Ragnarok.

JÖRMUNGANDR

One sketch often grows out of another. While working on a sketch of Ouroboros, he suddenly began to look very much like *Jörmungandr*, so I let myself get side-tracked. A word of advice: when some unlooked-for idea pops unbidden into your brain in the wake of some serendipitous stroke of the pencil when you *should* be concentrating on a different subject, *stop* what you're doing and sketch it out. It won't take long, and it may not come your way again. This is another image I see clearly in colour, so the extra effort shading in the water is to assuage my frustration at not being able to dive in right away with watercolours.

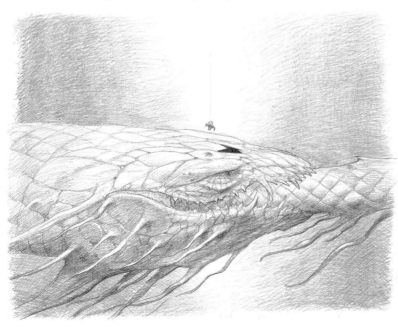

PAINTING THE WYRM

A couple of decades ago I visited one of those awful itinerant reptile exhibitions that set up their tents in town every now and then. I asked if I could take photos. 'I won't use a flash,' I reassured the owner, who replied, 'You can if you like, the snakes couldn't care less.' Naturally, I didn't use it, but steadied my lens against the glass of a grubby terrarium and photographed a boa constricted in a tank barely big enough for him to fold himself into. The place stank. But I came away with a series of photos that have been my foundation for Nidhoggr ever since.

Barring the blue spirals and the lifted head, my Nidhoggr is exactly that boa. Without getting all romantic about it, it's a perfect illustration of the chance meeting of object and subject, when the image in your head and the image in front of your eyes somehow coincide.

Snakes are not just long tapered sausages with heads. There is always a lot of energy packed into the body, and the backbone, ribs and muscles make it a symphony of intersecting forms and lines. Keeping in one's mind where that energy bunches up, where it relaxes and how the interplay of both contribute to the silhouette is important.

THE SCALE OF THINGS

Painting scales is something I generally do several times for any creature. Once the general tones are blocked in the first step is a set of criss-crossed lines that follow the shape of the body, done with a very full brush of water over a very wet ground of ink, or a brush full of ink over a lighter ground. (This doesn't work well with watercolour; inks are more reactive.) Often, I'll go over that again to give more shape to the general form, and only then start working up individual scales. The scales are done either by outlining them with darker lines, or using water to lift the ink from a darker ground – where two strokes of water cross, the spot will be much lighter. The final touch is to add the highlights: for this nothing beats gathering a series of reference photos.

ABOVE: THE BLIND WYRM

There are few animals I find positively repulsive, but lampreys come close. They seem to have no saving graces (of course they don't need my approval to lead happy lives, and I would never bother one) so they are naturally the inspiration for Nidhoggr's blind head and saw-toothed maw.

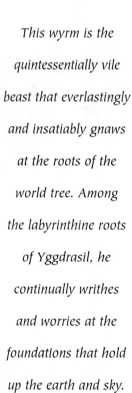

This wyrm is the
quintessentially vile
beast that everlastingly
and insatiably gnaws
at the roots of the
world tree. Among
the labyrinthine roots
of Yggdrasil, he
continually writhes
and worries at the
foundations that hold
up the earth and sky.

VOLCANIC DRAGONS

Dragons sometimes spit acid, frost or venom – and those who can speak generally have poison in their words – but most commonly, and most dramatically, they are fire-breathers. Born to the earth, they sleep for centuries in gloomy caverns under hills and mountains, but when they rouse themselves they are capable of bursting through earth's fragile skin to consume and destroy.

THE DEATH OF SMAUG

Smaug has set Lake Town alight and is now destroying the bridge for good measure. I spent quite a while wondering what wasn't working in the picture, until I finally realized that the smooth curving tail I had sketched in robbed Smaug of all energy and power. I broke that line by putting a small kink in his tail and suddenly everything fell into place.

Battling a living (and angry) flame-thrower is a dangerous game, but some heroes employ more brains than brawn. At the court of the Persian king Cyrus, the Hebrew prophet Daniel destroyed a dragon by tossing a ball of pitch, fat and hair into its mouth. It blew up. Others, like Beowulf, count on strength and their wide shields.

When Zeus fought and finally vanquished the hundred-headed fire-breathing serpent Typhoeus, earthquakes and tidal waves devastated the country round about. The last son of the earth goddess Gaea now sleeps uneasily, buried under Mount Etna in Sicily. When the monster erupts in anger he spews flame from his mouth and hurls red-hot rocks at the sky. If Vulcan is the Olympian god of volcanoes, personifying humankind's modest attempts to harness the power of fire in the forge, Typhoeus is the chthonic representation of vulcanism – raging, unpredictable, cataclysmic.

Arab astronomers used dragons as emblems for the stars, and comets were 'fiery dragons' trailing their glittering tails across the sky. But in fire-worshipping traditions such as Zoroastrianism, the dragon was the enemy of fire – the element that brought comfort and wisdom to the world. The Persian three-headed dragon Azi Dahaka waged war against the fire god Atar, trying to extinguish his flames; the dragon was eventually imprisoned under a mountain. Azi Dahaka was filled not with flame but with venom, like the poisonous wyrms of Norse mythology. In the West, dragons and fire began their long association in the early Middle Ages. The biblical vision of the Apocalypse irrevocably identified the dragon with the devil and sent it straight to Hell: its glowing, gaping jaws are often the mouth of Hell itself, spewing out flames and sulphur.

PAINTING FIRE

Fire is of course enormous fun to paint, as the structure is so subtle as to be almost an illusion in itself. I've always loved those slightly immaterial images of volcanoes that are reduced to totally mineral representations. They have the same beauty as images of traditional glassblowing or foundries (both of which I've had the opportunity to visit – the only thing missing on my list so far is charcoal burning, which is a spectacle straight out of Dante) – the transmutation of elements by fire into novel forms. All this amateur philosophy is to say that it's a theme I would love to revisit. Often. Oh, and of course I do need to visit an active volcano or two one day.

In this particular case, here is how it went (the image was done for a book on dragons and was intended to accompany the index, so it needed to accommodate long columns of text):

The first step in this kind of soft-toned approach is to get the whole picture going at once, ignoring only those portions in the foreground, which will be black, or darker elements that have their bases hidden by those features.

All the atmospheric elements – clouds, flames and sky – are done pretty much in one shot (which is generally about all you get at this kind of thing, otherwise the colours will lose their purity), without worrying too much about detail.

Next, if you've kept track of where you wished to put the actual dragons (more or less, because happenstance can dictate changes), they can be painted in, starting with the ones farthest away and working towards the front of the picture.

An effect worthwhile spending some time on is painting red edges where the yellows are brightest; it will make the darker elements feel much less flat. A little coloured pencil can be helpful to smooth things out when you're done, and works in areas that are just too hard to detail when working quickly with a large brush on a wet ground.

*When the
dragons sleeping
under the earth
have troubled
dreams, we
call them
earthquakes.
They awake as
volcanoes.*

MONSTERS & HEROES

Dragons and serpents are composites of all that is inhuman: fantastic, fearful size and strength, scales, claws, wings, flame and venom. Perhaps it was inevitable that they should prove the ultimate test of every warrior. A long tradition of stories about the vanquishing of dragons begins with gods and angels, but the more stirring tales are those of human heroes.

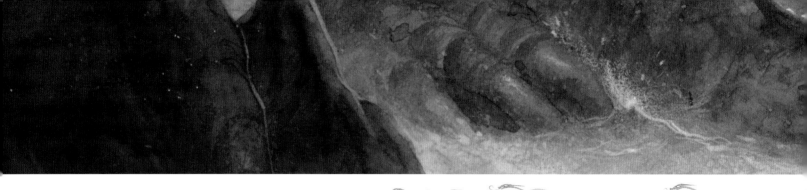

DRAGON ISLE

Dragons often issue forth from the earth, and may return to slumber there, for a year, for a thousand, or sometimes more. There are many legends of dragons sleeping for centuries in the earth, under mountains, hills and mounds. Sometimes the dragon IS the hill, its bony spine silhouetted against the sky and its snout resting on the plain below or in the sea. The landscape is peaceful so long as the beast rests undisturbed, but if it wakes the ground will tremble, shift and split.

VORTIGERN'S CASTLE
King Vortigern finds the red dragon of Wales and the white dragon of the Saxons fighting under his castle, from Wace's *Chronicles*, mid-14th century.

Landscape features with dragon legends attached can be found from the Great Orme (or 'worm') of North Wales to Yongdu-am ('Dragon Head Rock') in Jeju, South Korea. They are the perfect illustrations of the desire and need to make sense of occurrences beyond human understanding. Gradually, like all vast myths, they will affix themselves to salient features of the land. The magic returns to the earth, but in the case of dragon lore, it is often dangerous magic, slumbering but not dead, in the same way that the earth slumbers, only to tremble again when earthquakes strike. The heroes who subdue wyrms and exile them underground represent our courageous yet paltry efforts to prevail over the indomitable, if not by act, then by story. A famous Dragon Hill stands near the 3,000-year-old White Horse of Uffington in the south of England. This conical, flat-topped mound is said to be the site of St George's victory, and the spot where the dragon's blood was spilt can still be identified, since no grass ever grows there. Locals claim the chalk figure is in fact not a horse but a dragon, which will rise and dance on Dragon Hill at the return of Arthur, the once and future king.

Another story would have the hill to be a burial mound, an ancient barrow in which a dragon once guarded treasure. In the 10th century the hill was called 'Church Barrow', perhaps because a religious foundation had been built on an established pagan sacred site. Churches built in such places, as at Jellinge in Denmark, were invested with the spirituality of the old beliefs as well as the new doctrine.

The fighting dragons of England and Wales
The red dragon that appears on the Welsh flag was once buried under Dinas Emrys, a hill in Snowdonia. According to a story in the Mabinogion, it was locked in battle with the white dragon of the Saxons, and their screams caused panic among the people. Lludd, King of Britain, created a trap for them filled with mead: the dragons fell into a drunken stupor and were imprisoned under the hill. Centuries later, King Vortigern commanded a castle to

be built on the spot, but walls erected one day had toppled by the following morning. Vortigern's counsellors advised him to placate the local spirits by sacrificing a fatherless child. The boy he chose turned out to be the young wizard Merlin, who advised him instead to dig down beneath the foundations. The workmen found a pool, which Merlin instructed them to drain. At the bottom were the two dragons, who immediately renewed their battle. Eventually the red dragon triumphed and drove the white dragon out of Wales.

Dragons and dinosaurs

I'm not convinced of any real link between dinosaurs and dragons, nor do I find dinosaur anatomy to be a source of inspiration, but there is a clear family likeness between the terrible lizards of prehistory and those of our collective imagination. (This said, dinosaurs themselves have considerably evolved since I was small – a Tyrannosaurus Rex when I was six was a chubby, upright creature with a limp tail and a quizzical expression – a far cry from today's versions. Dragons are, thankfully, far less temporal.) Fossilized dinosaur remains dug up in China in 300 BC were classified as 'dragon bones', and are still so described (and in use, in traditional Chinese medicine). While cryptozoologists search for evidence of 'living fossils' such as the pterosaur-like ropen of Papua New Guinea, and Young Earth creationists argue that dinosaurs and humans co-existed before the Flood (Noah took dinosaur eggs and young dinosaurs aboard the Ark, since they took up less space), it's generally agreed that the age of the dinosaurs ended 65 million years ago – long before there were any human heroes to do battle with them or even retain some dim memory of them. Dinosaur bones were certainly not enough to have suggested the idea of the dragon in the first place, but they likely added force to many a legend before they were recognized for what they are. (The belief in giants was built on similar proof, before it was realized the bones were those of mammoths.)

WORM'S HEAD, RHOSSILI
This rocky outcrop, linked at low tide by a causeway to the mainland at the tip of the Gower Peninsula in South Wales, is unmistakably a basking dragon – about a mile long from nose to tail. Local legend has it that the sight deterred invading Vikings from landing here, and they were later shipwrecked in Swansea Bay. Topographical features like this are often stepping stones for the imagination.

SKETCHING THE DRAGONS

While this isn't intended as a course in dragon landscaping, such creatures are so closely tied to the earth and the forces that shape it that finding hints of dragon in rocks, hills and skylines is common enough to imagine that in a fantasy world, these creatures might be a little closer to the surface, so to speak, and a little easier to see. They also aptly raise the question of how to paint images where evocation takes precedent over description. Only a fine line divides the two.

DRAGON MOUNTAIN

What if a mountain range itself was a dragon asleep ... I'm not terribly pleased with the skull, which is far too realistic. It would also be far more effective in colour. Sometimes, though, especially in the case of landscapes, it's hard to know when to stop.

DRAGON'S SPINE VIGNETTE

From a novel by Robin Hobb: a traveller comes to a ridge of standing stones – the vertebrae of a dragon.

DRAGON ISLE SKETCH

I absolutely adore images of volcanoes spewing lava into the sea, and have a grand collection of photos that I haul out to gaze at just for the sheer beauty of the contrasts – wave, rock and liquid fire in a chromatic symphony of opposites. This was to be an excursion into that theme, for the simple pleasure of the colours and textures. In the end, I had to fall back on a rather tamer image that needed a calm clear sky and lower horizon to accommodate text. But I'll go back and do a wilder image one day. (Actually, I guess that is my most oft-used phrase. I rarely manage to actually do these pictures I so optimistically dream about. The road to illustration is paved with good intentions.)

Under a gathering storm lies a jagged and hostile
rocky shore: a living island, now in slumber, but
which might awake with the scrape of a boat's keel
or the sound of human voices.

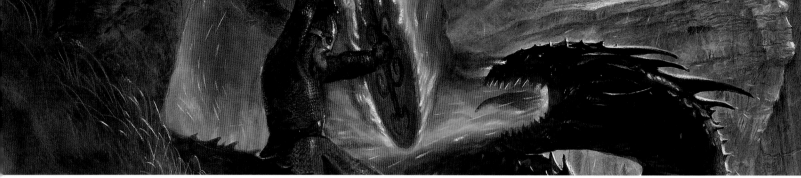

BEOWULF'S DRAGON

A dragon can raise mountains, eclipse the sun, swallow rivers and scorch the earth: to battle with this force of nature is the ultimate test for a human hero, and the figure of the dragon-slayer is as universal as the mythical beast itself. The encounter between Beowulf and the glittering, terrible dragon is a fight to the death for both man and monster.

In the epic Anglo-Saxon poem, composed some time between the seventh and tenth centuries, Beowulf is a Great prince (from a region now in southern Sweden) whose battles with three fearsome adversaries are the dramatic high points of the narrative. As a young man he journeys to the land of the Danes to rid them of the menacing creature Grendel, and subsequently of Grendel's mother. Then, after a 50-year reign over the Geats, he faces his final encounter, with a dragon terrorizing his own country. He succeeds in killing the dragon but is fatally wounded.

Despite the poem's Christian perspective, its characters inhabit a pagan Germanic world in which blood feuds are pursued by the warring tribes of Swedes, Danes and Geats, and just as remorselessly by the monsters: Grendel's mother must have revenge for the attack on her son, and the dragon, waking after three centuries, can't wait to go on the rampage to avenge the loss of his treasure. For Beowulf himself, vengeance is preferable to mourning, and the glory of victory is the key to immortality.

Treasure, specifically gold, embodies that glory and crops up throughout the narrative, with detailed descriptions of jewels and weaponry such as the finely wrought helmet, chain mail and precious torque King Hrothgar gives to Beowulf. In our own time the significance of such things is familiar to readers of Tolkien, whose warriors share the values of Beowulf's world. The king is described as 'ring-giver' and 'gold-friend'; an ancient sword is like a fellow warrior, honoured with a name and empowered by the heroic deeds it once accomplished. A code of honour governs the possession of riches: Beowulf finds a hoard in Grendel's mother's lair but will not take it, and when he returns home he presents the spoils he has earned to his king. The importance of treasure is in the giving and right ownership, not in hoarding, and it's considered a fitting motive for vengeance when it falls into the wrong hands.

VIKING DRAGON

A carved wooden post of about 850, found at Oseberg in Norway, from a Viking ship burial of the kind described in the opening lines of *Beowulf*.

BEOWULF MANUSCRIPT

The opening page of the only known medieval copy of the poem, written in the early 11th century. Acquired by the antiquarian Sir Robert Cotton in the 17th century, it survived the fire that ravaged his library only after being thrown out of a window.

Dragons, like gold, infest the poem. The minstrel's song that celebrates Beowulf's victory over Grendel is all about the Norse hero Sigemund killing a dragon, a story that prefigures Beowulf's own battle to come. Beowulf's tales of his youthful exploits include a raid on a nest of trolls and the killing of nine sea monsters. Grendel's mother's gloomy mere is haunted by angry sea-dragons and wyrms: Beowulf kills one of them bloodily. And Grendel's curious glove or pouch, in which he keeps chunks of his victims in case he feels hungry, is made of dragon skins.

The dragon Beowulf has to face in his old age is disturbed from its long sleep when a thief steals a jewelled goblet from its lair. For centuries it has guarded the treasure of an ancient race, buried by its

BEOWULF: THE DRAGON'S RAMPAGE
The dragon, woken from its slumber by a thief stealing a cup from its hoard, ravages the countryside. Even when not breathing fire, it is so hot that the earth smoulders and sparks under its coils.

last survivor. Powered by watchfulness and greed, the dragon knows every item of its hoard; it instantly misses the goblet and will not rest until it is recovered. It wreaks havoc, burning everything in its path as it goes on the rampage each night. But in its furious quest for vengeance it is simply following the same code as everyone else in the world of the poem.

BEOWULF'S BATTLE WITH THE DRAGON

The hero Beowulf has proved his superhuman prowess in the epic battles of his youth. When he faces the dragon, however, he is an old man, still strong, but now full of foreboding. The dragon is far older – an ancient creature woken from centuries of sleep. And seeking revenge.

Beowulf's world turns on the warrior's honour, glory in battle and the pursuit of vengeance, and he knows that blood feuds must be pursued to their bitter end. Even for a trifle from a dragon's vast hoard – a golden cup, a fistful of coins – revenge must be exacted. The dragon cannot be placated. It must be destroyed. There must be battle, even though the old king knows it will be his last. He puts it off, like an old warrior who hopes spring will ease the ache of old wounds, but when the dragon comes, he must respond.

Against fire he has no weapons, so he has an iron shield forged to resist the dragon's flames. He goes to seek out the monster in its own lair, in the barrow by the sea. When the dragon emerges, belching fire, it recognizes the power of its enemy and the fight begins on equal terms. But Beowulf's sword – not his courage or his aim – fails him, splintering on the dragon's skull. All but one of his followers flee as he is wreathed in a shroud of fire. Only Wiglaf stays loyal and hacks the dragon with his ancient sword. The flames subside, but the dragon's venomous teeth are already in Beowulf's neck. He kills the beast with his knife, stabbing from below into its more vulnerable flank and throat. Beowulf sends Wiglaf into the barrow to bring out the dragon's hoard so that he can see it before he dies, and bequeaths it to his people. They will bury the treasure with their king, so dear is the price they have paid for it. The vast carcass of the dragon, twenty-five alens long and scorched and blackened by its own flames, is tossed unceremoniously into the sea.

PAINTING THE DRAGON

The initial sketches I did for a boardgame box cover were judged to give too much importance to the dragon. The editor requested that the roles be reversed.

FIRST VERSION
The initial sketches showed Beowulf crouching behind his shield, wreathed by an inferno of flame. The publisher wanted Beowulf, rather than his opponent, to dominate the scene.

SECOND VERSION
I turned things around, but lost my concentration on the dragon, briefly toying with the idea of putting wings on him. Even if the sketch wasn't going quite right, it served to sort out the various elements.

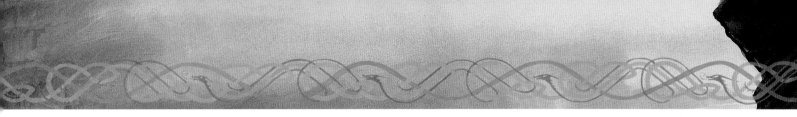

BEOWULF AND THE DRAGON

The dragon's lair, under a rocky cliff lashed by the sea, is a dark, remote location of fear and horror.

Beowulf grips his sword like a knife: for stabbing only, not thrusting or cutting. That detail, more than any other, hints at the desperation of his struggle.

DETAIL OF THE BATTLE

I drew the scene directly onto stretched paper, keeping most of the dragon (especially the vigorous lines of the tail) and redrawing Beowulf until he found the right position, with his shield held straight out at arm's length. Most of the serious thinking revolved around getting the flames to work to my satisfaction. With a flame-throwing dragon, burning grass, a blazing shield and contrary winds, there was quite a lot of combustion to think about.

Beowulf's final struggle is a wrenching horrid grapple on sharp, wet rocks, choking on the dragon's fumes. No swordplay either: his blade is a butcher's knife, hacking and stabbing. Only the protection of his shield will allow him to survive long enough to take his foe with him into death.

FAFNIR

T he dragon Fafnir was originally a dwarf. His greed, though, his dark love of bright gold and glittering jewels and his gnawing fear that thieves might steal them, so ate at his soul that it transformed his body. His belly dragged on the earth, scales and wicked spikes grew from his spine, his crooked limbs grew great talons. Fafnir became a dragon with fire smouldering in his poisonous blood and a deep hatred of all things in his heart, equal only to his greed. The theme of transformation, often as the result of a curse, occurs repeatedly in dragon myth and folklore.

SIGURD KILLS FAFNIR
This carved portal of the 12th-century wooden stave church at Hyllestad in Norway, depicts scenes from the story of Sigurd and Fafnir, using the pagan hero as a symbol of Christ subduing the devil.

The dwarf Hriedmar has three sons: Fafnir, Otr and Regin. While Fafnir and Regin are drawn to the fires of their father's forge, Otr prefers the water, swimming and catching fish with the suppleness of an otter. Loki the trickster god kills Otr, mistaking him for the otter he so resembles. Pressed by Hriedmar for bloodgeld, Loki offers to fill the otter skin with gold, but includes in it a ring engraved with a curse of greed. Fafnir, lusting after the gold, conspires with Regin to steal it, and together they kill their father Hriedmar. To defend his treasure and to avoid sharing with his sibling, Fafnir (whose name means 'embracer') finally takes the form of a monstrous wingless dragon.

Regin's desire for the treasure is just as great, so he persuades his foster-son, Sigurd (or, in his German guise, Siegfried), to kill the dragon. Regin forges the great sword Gram, and advises Sigurd to dig a pit in Fafnir's customary path to the river to drink (to quench, even briefly, the eternal thirst provoked by the fiery greed smouldering in his heart) and thrust the sword into the great wyrm's belly as he passes over it. Odin, in his earthly guise of wandering one-eyed greybeard, offers more advice. He cautions Sigurd to bathe in Fafnir's blood, as it will make him invulnerable. Sigurd follows his advice and slays the dragon. He bathes in the creature's blood, and becomes invulnerable, except for one small spot on his shoulder, where a leaf has stuck. Regin wishes to eat Fafnir's heart, knowing it will confer wisdom, so Sigurd cuts it out and cooks it. In doing so he burns his finger: instinctively he licks it, and the dragon's blood gives him the power to understand the language of the birds. Their songs warn Sigurd that his foster-father is planning to kill him. Sigurd kills Regin and takes the gold, but the curse is still at work.

Shape-shifters and transformations

Fafnir's avarice is so great that it subsumes both his character and his appearance: he becomes a dragon, the archetype of greed.

The transformation of human into dragon is usually the result of a curse. In the Northumbrian folktale known as 'The Laidly Worm' ('laidly' meaning 'loathsome') a princess is turned into a dragon by her wicked stepmother. Her brother, however, dares to kiss the repulsive creature three times. The princess is released from the malediction, which backfires on the stepmother, who turns into a toad. The story is set in Bamburgh Castle, and local girls would avoid the beach below the keep for fear of meeting the monstrous toad and suffering the princess's fate.

The fantastical 14th-century *Travels of Sir John Mandeville* includes the sad story of the 'Lady of the Land', a beautiful woman transformed into a dragon living in a cave on the Greek island of Lango, or Cos. One simple kiss would lift the curse, but though men visit the cave, attracted by her land and wealth, none can bring himself to kiss her and every one is killed.

THE DRAGON WITHIN

This sketch was done for the Beowulf movie during the (very) brief time I worked on pre-production. The dragon Beowulf battles is actually his own son, so I imagined that the shape-changing scene would not be one of those painful joint-cracking, skin-stretching moments where effects teams go to town, but a shimmering, floating, blurring and shifting of outlines until the dragon within leaps into focus.

PAINTING THE DRAGON

Quite frankly, digging a shallow pit in the path of a poisonous and gigantic dragon is a brave thing to try. The painting on the following pages is not one I really care for very much, but it does have the merit of showing clearly what *not* to do…

I wanted to contrast the idyllic forest scene with the tension of Sigurd's ambush, but I didn't do the woodland to my satisfaction and don't care much for the dragon either. (Sigurd is all right – a meagre consolation.) All in all, I was hesitating between priorities and that can be as dangerous as waiting in a shallow pit in the path of a poisonous and gigantic dragon…

THE TRANSFORMING OF FAFNIR
Wouldn't this feel just awful? The changing of physical form to mirror a darkening of the soul is common enough in fantasy art. I will try to capture some of the anguish and ambiguity in his eyes when it is time to do the colour piece. (It's also a fair likeness of me – nothing like throwing yourself into your work…)

SIGURD AND FAFNIR

Another stab (appropriately) at Fafnir, this time focusing on Sigurd. For the colour illustration I will move the dragon's head farther left and make the neck longer.

PAINTING DETAIL

I can barely look at this dragon without wincing, which is hardly the kind of admission one enjoys making. How I wish I had spent more time sketching out the dragon rather than just pulling the pointy head out of my hat. (I probably succumbed to mounting deadline panic.) Actually, I would have been wise to draw the dragon in his entirety – well, perhaps not the tail, but the body at the very least – to place him properly. The moral of the story is that it's a *very* wise idea to draw what will not be visible in the final artwork. (See? I knew there was something worthwhile in there after all.)

Following the

treacherous Regin's

plan, Sigurd has dug

a hollow in the track

worn by the dragon

Fafnir as he comes

to quench his thirst

at a river. Now he

prepares to strike.

ST GEORGE'S DRAGON

 Though we hardly know whether he really existed, St George is the most eminent of a host of dragon-slaying saints. His image is universally familiar, equipped with his shining armour and his white horse, plunging his lance into the throat of the cowering monster. But it was not until centuries after his martyrdom that the dragon became part of his story.

The earliest versions of the dragon-slaying narrative concern battles between an ancient serpent and a solar deity – such as the Babylonian Tiamat and the god Marduk. The Archangel Michael shares the attributes of the solar hero, and defeats Satan in the guise of a seven-headed dragon, imprisoning him in a bottomless pit. St George's princess seems to have been inherited from classical versions of the story, in which Perseus kills a sea monster to save the Phoenician princess Andromeda, and Heracles kills another to rescue the Trojan king Laomedon's daughter Hesione.

THE HERALDIC DRAGON

The engraved silver seal die of Robert Fitzwalter from the early 13th century shows the knight in combat with a dragon, aligning him with the military saints and affirming his Christian faith. The heraldic dragon symbolized nobility and courage as it was considered a worthy opponent for a knight.

The legend tells that George was born in the late 3rd century at Lydda, and served in the imperial guard of Diocletian, but when the emperor authorized the extermination of Christians, he opposed it and was tortured and beheaded. He was canonized in 494, but his cult really blossomed in the Middle Ages, when his military status, stand against paganism, and Palestinian origins made him a natural patron of the Crusaders. He gained additional heraldic glamour and patron sainthood in England when the Order of the Garter was dedicated to his honour in 1348.

Arriving in Europe with the returning Crusaders, St George somehow acquired a dragon along the way. As usual with dragons, it has a connection with water: it lives at the spring that supplies the city of Silene, and the inhabitants have to find a way to distract it while they collect water. This they do by offering it a daily sacrifice of sheep. When all the sheep are gone they offer children, chosen by lot. On the day that George rides by, the lot has fallen to the king's daughter. George fights the dragon and rescues the princess. The dragon allows itself to be led meekly into the town on a leash, and George promises the citizens that he will kill it if they become Christians. They eagerly agree. The dragon is promptly despatched and a church built on the site. A healing spring gushes from its altar.

St George is one of many saints doing battle with dragons in allegories of Christianity conquering paganism. Another is St Martha, who tames the French dragon, the Tarasque, with holy water and a crucifix. (It demurely accompanies her into the town of Nerluc in Provence, where it is, somewhat harshly, stoned to death.) St Martha goes on to

BANNER FOR THE COMPANY OF SAINT GEORGE
A St George (and mandatory dragon) done in oils on damask for a replica of a late 15th-century banner. Painted with pigments simply mixed with oil, it took absolutely ages to dry, and the rather generous tail of George's steed covers a spot where the paint bled through the cloth.

convert the townspeople; regretting their unchristian treatment of the beast, they rename the town Tarascon in its memory.

St George flourishes in stone, wood and paint throughout medieval Europe. When he is not mounted on his charger, lance couched at a charge, he is often shown despatching a tiny lizard-like dragon the size of a small spaniel pinned down by one iron-clad foot, while preparing to puncture it with his lance or chop it into slices with raised sword. This curious disproportion is rectified with the Renaissance, which sees a classically armoured George pitted against writhing beasts more akin to crocodiles than lap dogs.

ST MICHAEL

This is the start of what promises to be a long series of sketches of St Michael. Being an archangel as well as a saint, he deserves a rather more hieratic treatment than his more demotic saintly colleagues. Medieval paintings often show Michael in full golden gothic armour, which was my intention here, with a backdrop of writhing dragon. (I was happiest with my idea of fixing his slightly inconvenient wings on his greaves – much time can be wasted worrying about silly dilemmas such as how to reconcile a full back plate and huge white pinions.)

ST GEORGE'S DRAGON

SKETCHING THE DRAGON

This picture is a study in contrast between the idyllic forest setting and the pitching, thrashing, roiling mass of the dragon, encumbered by the trees, with St George madly dashing about lopping off bits where he can. The image is contained by the three main trees, which pin the action in place. Otherwise, this illustration is entirely within the category of those that are 'safe bets'. Once the general tone is set, it is really just a question of working from back to front in the image.

THE DRAGON

Often when I'm sketching a dragon, I'll end up with a welter of flailing limbs and lashing tails cluttering up my page as ideas pile up. When all those possibilities have been put on paper (or when I just can't make anything out any more), it's usually enough to work from without further sketching on the finished piece – at some point one option in the turmoil of overlapping ideas seems like the right one and is resolved with an energetic stroke of a brush well filled with paint.

LIGHT AND DARK

St George, with his bright shield emblazoned with its red cross, is a very intrusive element, especially given my reluctance to deal decisively with brighter colours. (I did the best I could at the time with the costume and weaponry; I'd do it much differently now.)

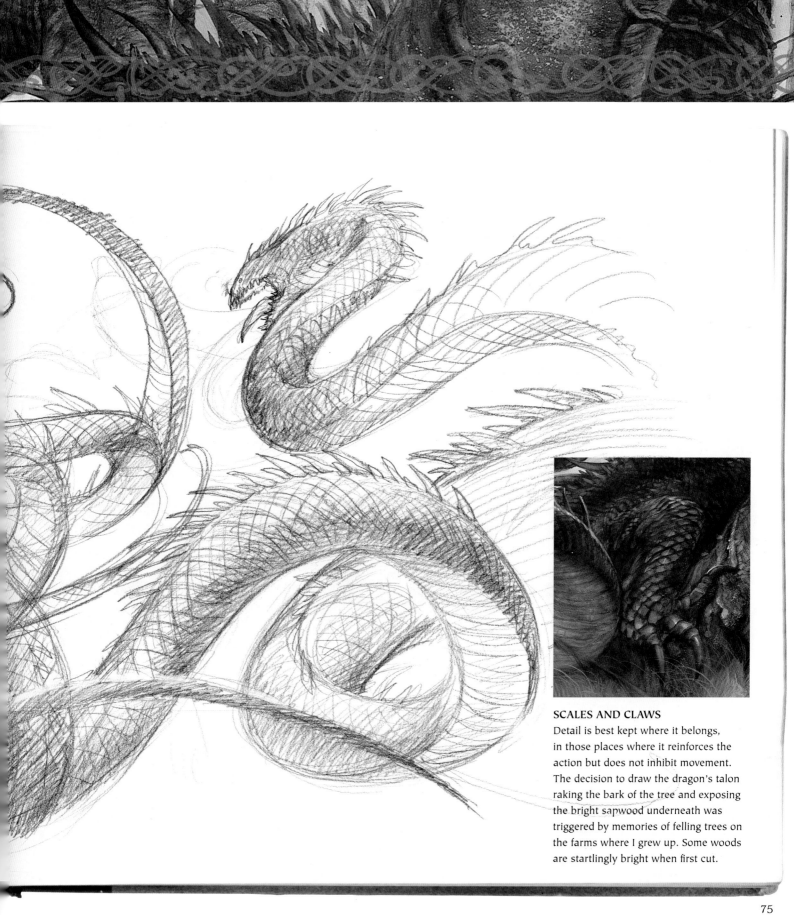

SCALES AND CLAWS

Detail is best kept where it belongs, in those places where it reinforces the action but does not inhibit movement. The decision to draw the dragon's talon raking the bark of the tree and exposing the bright sapwood underneath was triggered by memories of felling trees on the farms where I grew up. Some woods are startlingly bright when first cut.

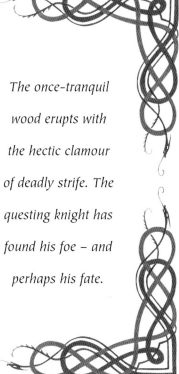

The once-tranquil wood erupts with the hectic clamour of deadly strife. The questing knight has found his foe – and perhaps his fate.

LANCELOT'S DRAGON

In medieval romance literature, the knights who ride out of castle gates are travelling in search of adventure into an unknown world, a desert where they expect to meet giants, enchanters and venomous monsters. They are out to win fame and fortune, and the killing of a dragon is an essential feature of the aspiring knight's quest. Naturally, Lancelot, one of the greatest of the Arthurian knights-errant, faces a dragon of his own.

The known medieval world was both a smaller and a larger realm than the world we know today. Far smaller, as the earth had yet to be circumnavigated and fully mapped, far larger because beyond the known borders, imagination provided a speculative patchwork of extraordinary realms. Mapmakers filled the margins and *terra incognita* of their mappamundi with fantastic and fanciful creatures. The Atlantic Ocean of the Middle Ages and the Renaissance was dotted with mythical isles, from Hy Brazil to the Isle of Demons, and between them, sea serpents and monsters crawled the waves. The offspring of Leviathan shared the deeps with confused or incomplete stories of sea snakes large enough to swallow whales, or devil-whales big enough to resemble islands. (Indeed, unwary mariners might anchor alongside such phenomena, and go ashore. If they made themselves comfortable by building a fire, it would awaken the sleeping creature, which would devour them and their unfortunate vessel.)

Unknown continents, if they were home to unicorns and preposterous creatures such as giraffes or barely creditable races of pygmies or giants, certainly harboured dragons. In India and Ethiopia,

dragons were said to be the mortal enemies of elephants. Tales such as the Voyage of St Brendan and the very real travels of the brothers Polo, William of Rubruck or Ibn Battuta, spawned ideas of dragons and other dangerous beasts across the world. Near the east coast of Africa, on the Lenox Globe constructed in the early 16th century, the cartographer penned '*Hc svnt draconis*' – 'Here be dragons' – a phrase we use still, a picturesque shorthand for dangerous, unfamiliar places, peopled with unexpected creatures.

The bestiaries of the medieval illuminators were vivid collections of animals that freely mixed up the real and the imaginary, drawing on observations of animal behaviour but also on classical treatises, the Bible and stories of variable accuracy gleaned from travellers returning from Asia and Africa. Bestiaries, whether assembled in manuscripts or leering at passers-by from lofty cathedrals, not only satisfied a secular yearning for the marvellous, but served a religious purpose. The creatures were allegories, with characteristics that illustrated points of theology or offered moral guidance. Serpents stood for evil, as they did in the Bible, and the dragon, as the greatest of serpents, represented Satan, the greatest evil. The commentaries described a dragon killing an elephant by suffocating it in its coils in order to show how the devil entangled people in sin. The dragon was also the enemy of the panther, which was portrayed as a gentle beast with sweet breath: a symbol of Christ.

JAVELIN SNAKES
First mentioned by Lucan and Pliny, jaculi or javelin snakes were described by Isidore of Seville in the 7th century in his *Etymologies*: 'The jaculus is a flying snake. They jump from trees and dart on to passing animals, from which they get their name, "darter"'.

A MAP OF AFRICA

The first-century Roman naturalist Pliny the Elder had asserted that dragons 'twenty cubits in length' inhabited Ethiopia, and this detail of the Genoese World Map of 1457 shows that they were still associated with the region.

A DRAGON TRAPS AN ELEPHANT

In a late 13th-century manuscript, *Dicta chrysostomi*, a winged dragon coils its tail around the legs of its traditional enemy, the elephant. The bestiarists claimed that the dragon sucked the cool blood of the elephant to refresh it in the parching desert heat.

LANCELOT'S DRAGON

The questing knight

A fanciful landscape of monsters and magic is the setting for medieval romance, a tradition in which Sir Lancelot, orphaned and raised by the mysterious Lady of the Lake in ignorance of his noble lineage, is the epitome of the knight-errant, undertaking a long succession of adventures to prove his valour and gallantry.

In the course of his wanderings he comes to Corbenic, the castle of the Holy Grail, where Elaine, the daughter of King Pelles, is magically trapped in a tub of scalding water, awaiting rescue by the best of all knights. Having freed her, he is led to a cemetery where an inscription on a tombstone prophesies that only the greatest of knights will be able to lift it, and that he will father a lion born to the daughter of the King of the Land Beyond. Though not understanding the prophecy he easily lifts the stone, and a fire-breathing dragon is released. Everyone flees in terror, but Lancelot, sheltering from the flames behind his shield, attacks and kills the monster. Elaine falls in love with Lancelot and entices him into her bed by enchantment. The child they conceive will be Galahad, the lion of the prophecy and the perfect knight, destined to find the Grail.

Sir Tristan is another paragon of chivalry who wins a lady by killing a dragon. Hearing that Ireland is plagued by a rampaging dragon and that the king's daughter Isolde will be won by whoever rids the kingdom of the beast, he sets out to slay it. He is very nearly overwhelmed, but, finally killing the monster, he cuts out its venomous tongue and puts it inside his shirt. He stumbles to a nearby pond to drink but, exhausted from the fight and overcome by the poisonous emanations from the creature's tongue, he collapses and lies unconscious in the shallows. Meanwhile, the King's seneschal, who wants Isolde for himself, comes across the carcass of the dragon; he and his henchmen sever the creature's head and return in triumph. But Isolde finds Tristan and nurses him back to health. He confronts the deceitful seneschal, produces the missing tongue and claims Isolde.

TRISTAN AND ISOLDE
By killing a dragon Tristan wins the hand of Isolde for his uncle, King Mark of Cornwall. But as he escorts her from Ireland the two become lovers after mistakenly drinking a love potion that in some versions of the story is said to be made from dragon's blood.

THE RED CROSS KNIGHT

The white dragon in the distance is of course impossibly huge, almost more of an illusion or mirage than a real dragon. In a way, it is also the illusion of chivalry, the last quests into an age of fantasy before the ineluctable advent of the modern world – an illusion that recedes as fast as one can approach.

PAINTING THE DRAGON

While the focus of this Lancelot is of course the armour (any excuse will suffice) I wanted to convey the vulgarity and sadness in seeing a fantastical creature transformed by a zealous armoured juggernaut into a lifeless carcass, devoid even of the opportunity for a 'big game' souvenir photo. The poor thing has no more appeal than a dead eel and didn't stand much more of a chance. This isn't real gothic armour, it's a 19th-century copy, but it fitted me very well and I had a friend take photos of me from every angle. I won't write the painting off by saying, 'It's easy, just dig up a decent photo and copy it slavishly,' but that is basically what I did.

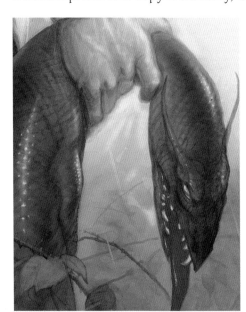

ADDING HIGHLIGHTS
The dead dragon, besides being small, is actually quite delicate with fine scales. Doing the highlights means choosing a line and highlighting with a scalpel the scales that fall on that line and then working the edges of the surrounding scales that face it from both sides. Once that's done, I like to run over it with a very hard eraser (the ones that are like pencils, with eraser instead of lead) to blur the hard edges and warm up the light.

DEAD DRAGON
The sketch is very much driven by memories of fishing off the coast of British Columbia. My father (an avid fisherman and a fearless navigator in his tiny rowing boat) was *very* late returning one afternoon, but turned up with a fifty-pound lingcod. I was at home visiting that summer so of course took dozens of photos, which have been a considerable aid in drawing awful, limp, slimy, cold, dead things ever since.

All the glamour and romance of the peerless knight's battle with a fire-breathing dragon have vanished now that it is reduced to a cumbersome corpse.

MELUSINE

The lovely Melusine insisted on privacy when taking her bath on a Saturday. For many years she guarded the secret of her serpent self, but when her husband discovered it she flew away and was only ever seen again as a winged dragon portending death. There were other she-dragons too, descendants of the ancient serpent goddess, who had the power to persuade men to see them only as beautiful and seductive women.

Stories of female dragons are of two kinds. There are legends of virtuous women transformed by enchantment into hideous monsters and eventually freed, with luck, by the power of love. Then there are others, of a much more ancient lineage, about serpent-women who control their own destinies. It's easy to see male anxiety and misogyny in the portrayal of seductive and powerful women as serpents from the waist down.

In Egypt, Minoan Crete, early Hinduism and other ancient cultures, a fecund earth goddess was worshipped before the emergence of male solar deities. She was revered in serpent form, and the suppression of her cult meant that the serpent came to be equated with evil. In the Bible it became the tempter of Eve, and the serpent of Eden was often portrayed with a woman's face, identifying it with the shadowy figure of Lilith, Adam's first wife.

Genesis includes two versions of the creation of man, and according to the first, he and the woman were made at the same time. Around this grew up the Hebrew legend of Lilith, who considered herself Adam's equal and refused to submit to his will, preferring to leave Eden and live in the desert. She acquired the character of a demon who killed babies and seduced men; she was identified with the night, vampirism and lust.

The Greek monster Lamia had a similar reputation, and was usually depicted as a beautiful woman with a serpent's tail. Hera had killed Lamia's children because she slept with Zeus, and in revenge she devoured the children of others and preyed on men. Hera condemned her to keep her eyes always open, until Zeus gave her the power to remove them from their sockets when she wished. There is an echo of this in the description of the French wyvern, the Vouivre, who also has a woman's body and a serpent's tail, and is a large, fire-breathing, treasure-hoarding dragon. Her single eye is a large ruby in her forehead, which she removes when she bathes. This makes her vulnerable: if it is stolen she is left blind and defenceless.

In another version of the myth, Lamia is a serpent enchantress who transforms herself into a woman to woo a youth. He is taken in and marries her, but she is recognized as a serpent by his tutor; this breaks the spell, and she reverts to her hideous real form.

The dragons of French folklore, such as the Tarasque and the Drac, are invariably associated with water. It was said that baby dragons were raised in rivers, nursed by mortal mothers who had been dragged into the water. Melusine herself is a water sprite who is finally transformed into a dragon. Unlike others of her kind she was loved, not loathed, and became the legendary matriarch of the Lusignan dynasty of Poitou and the Crusader kingdoms.

THE QUEEN OF THE NIGHT
This Babylonian relief of a winged and taloned deity from around 1950 BC has sometimes been identified as Lilith or Lilitu, a demoness sent by the goddess Ishtar to prey on men and lead them astray, though its iconography may link her more firmly with Ishtar herself.

THE HERALDIC MELUSINE

Heraldry conflated the serpent-tailed water fairy Melusine with the fish-tailed mermaid, and applied her name to a double-tailed form, always shown holding one tail in each hand.

MELUSINE FLIES AWAY

A woodcut from *La Liure de Mélusine en Fracoys*, published in 1478. Jean d'Arras wrote his very popular version of the story at the instigation of Jean, duc de Berry, to glorify the Lusignan dynasty.

The romance of Melusine

Elynas, king of Albany, fell in love with the fairy Pressyne; she agreed to marry him on condition that he would never try to see her when she was giving birth, but in his excitement he forgot his promise and rushed into the room. Pressyne was forced to leave the kingdom, taking her three lovely daughters, Melusine, Melior and Palatyne.

When she grew up, Melusine determined to seek revenge on her father for forcing them into exile. She and her sisters locked him in a mountain cave, but Pressyne was furious at their disrespect and cursed Melusine: she would be transformed into a serpent from the waist down every Saturday; the man she married must promise never to look at her on that day, and if he broke his vow she would be condemned to immortality in serpent form.

While out hunting, Raymond of Poitou came upon Melusine sitting by a fountain, and fell in love with her. He agreed to her condition that he must never see her on a Saturday, and they were married. In a single night Melusine built the great castle of Lusignan and they lived happily for many years, while she magically constructed fortresses and towns across Poitou. They had ten children, all strong and talented, though each suffered from some deformity: one, the violent-tempered Geoffrey, had a great tooth like a boar's tusk.

Raymond's relatives teased him about his wife's Saturday seclusion and eventually he became so suspicious that he spied on her through a crack in the door. He was horrified to see the coils of a great serpent's tail, but he loved Melusine and said nothing, until Geoffrey picked a fight with his brother and killed him, together with a hundred monks. Then Raymond blamed Melusine for contaminating his line with her serpent blood, and she knew that he had broken his vow. Transformed into a winged serpent, she flew over the castle roof three times, wailing bitterly, then disappeared, leaving her husband heartbroken. From time to time she would return, flying over the rooftops with terrible cries, and each appearance presaged the death of a Lord of Lusignan.

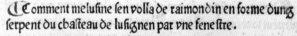

PAINTING THE DRAGON

The painting was part of a book of dragons; I very much wanted to vary the style and do a picture with an illustrative border. When working with traditional materials, this requires a considerable amount of taping off of borders and basically hoping that colour will not leak under the tape.

I can't look at this image without remembering where each element came from: the wall painting from a 12th-century French castle, the wooden bathing tub from a medieval manuscript, and the bench, jug and glass from my re-enactment gear. (The castle in the border illustration is Chillon, on Lake Geneva.)

After putting down an initial warm but very light wash, I masked off Melusine and the tub, in order to work up the wall with a wide brush and then paint in the fresco of the hunters. The rest was just concentrating on rendering the light and the reflected light on her body, reserving the darker tones for the less reflective surfaces. Suggesting the volumes by 'wrapping' the light around them is far more satisfying than images whose edges are simply too crisp and flat. Coloured pencils come in handy to soften the hard edges left by masking with tape.

As she rises from her enchanted bath, the faery Melusine reveals the secret she guards behind her closed chamber door each Saturday: a scaly serpent's tail.

MELUSINE SKETCH

One tail or two? Medieval representations of mermaids with two tails are very stylized, and transposing their anatomy into a realistic image is not always comfortable or even desirable. For the painting opposite I sidestepped the issue and hid what I wasn't sure how to draw. This version is a rather wilder Melusine, closer to her French cousin, the Vouivre.

DRAGONS OF OTHER WORLDS

Over the last century dragons have been to some extent redeemed. Folklore equated them with greed, malice and violence, and they suffered an increasingly bad press. But modern fantasy writers have rediscovered the more positive aspects of dragons – their wisdom and sensory super-powers. They remain unpredictable and dangerous, but some have formed alliances with humans, and all are glorious in their power.

WANDERING FIRE

 n a crowded earth, colossal, fire-breathing monsters might find it hard to hide, though mountaintops, deserts and jungles could still shelter unknown species, but the oceans are harder for humans to explore, and the deepest water could hold a creature of unimaginable size. Even a lake can be so deep as to be thought bottomless. Anything could be out there, or down there.

The sea is powerful, unpredictable, threatening, mysterious. In the beginning, the world was a world of water, an image of chaos populated with dragons and serpents of unthinkable size. When the earliest explorers ventured out to sea to find the limits of the world, who knew what they might find? And who was there to disprove the fantastic stories they told if they returned? A frail wooden ship, out of sight of land and tossed like a toy on the swell, might as well be the victim of a vast serpent lurking just below the waves.

They were primed by biblical tales of Leviathan, 'the dragon of the sea', who had existed from the fifth day of creation as a symbol of chaos subdued by God. The heat issuing from his mouth could make the sea boil and his jaws were described as the gates of hell. Hebrew tradition had it that on Judgment Day the righteous would feast on Leviathan's flesh, sitting in a tent made from his skin. Scandinavian fishermen terrified each other with stories of the Kraken, a monster so huge its back could be mistaken for an island, who sank ships in the whirlpool it created when it dived. It was worth the risk, though, as the waters where it rose heaved with fish.

Sightings of sea serpents of all sizes and shapes have been recounted in mariners' tales since antiquity. Rather than being pretexts to claim the existence of actual sea creatures, they are witness to the readiness of the imagination to shape the unexplained. Their power of evocation lies in the depths we can never explore – the ocean depths and the depth of our vision of the marvellous.

SEA DRAGON
I've always adored those wonderful photos (they seem to be everywhere) of lighthouses with impossibly huge waves practically submerging them. That was my starting point for this image, which was designed as a double spread requiring room for much text.

SEA SERPENT

A much more lizard-like dragon than I habitually do, painted to illustrate a book on dragons.

THE LIVESHIP VIVACIA

Sea snakes or dragons are an integral part of the cycle of dragon life in Robin Hobb's *Liveship Trilogy*, though initially, no connection is made between these dangerous saltwater snakes and the mythical race of dragonkind.

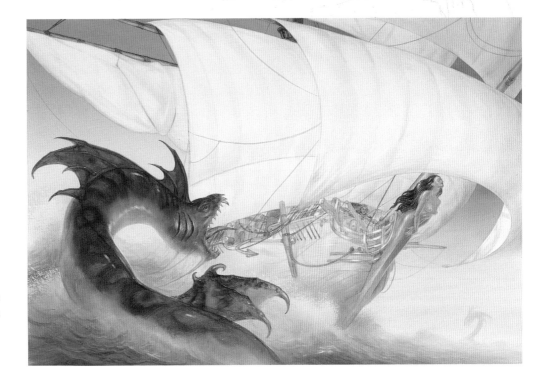

PAINTING THE SERPENT

I recall reading through a practically interminable Tolkien-like book, before finally deciding on this scene near the end. As with all full wraparound covers, all the action in this painting takes place in the lower right-hand portion of the image. I sketched out the elements separately – sea serpent's head and neck, ship, emerging coil with fin and finally the tail – and moved them about the page until they seemed to work. This is one of those images that involves the possibility of many, many things going wrong around several elements that simply cannot be moved once they have taken up their allotted stations.

THE SEA MONSTER

The creature turned out much better in the colour version than in the sketch. The difference is often very slight between a silhouette that works and one that is rather wooden and contrived. If something is nagging you in an initial sketch, it will often resolve itself when you pass from pencil to colour. Conversely, you can lose something you felt worked, but experience tells me that if you use your brushes freely without pencilling in too much, you will find it again.

The general tone went in first, mostly light blues and sea greens. Then the ship's stern and sail – even the pennant – were masked off with tape and a good deal of masking fluid was splattered about in stages, each time working down from the sky to the fore.

The sky went in next (minus the sun, which was added at the end), working down to the waves, and over the cresting wave near the creature's head until the sky was more or less in place.

Next came the foam at the spot where the tail emerges, and the spray between the boat and the creature's head, each element being completed before the masking fluid could be removed.

Next, the ship itself was cleared for action, and masking agent re-applied. (Remember, there was a light blue wash everywhere, not enough to kill any colours, but sufficient to remove the flat white glare of the paper.) The boat and sail meant masking with tape over the already finished background, the junctions near the waterline of the ship being blended out later.

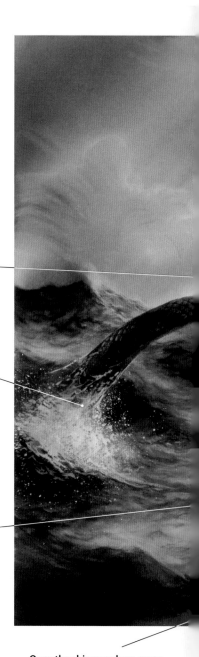

Once the ship was done, more masking fluid was spattered in front of the fin and back of the sea serpent, and that portion of his body worked in.

Last but not least (very much not least) was the sun – done with a hard eraser – and the light on the waves. Scraping away the colour resulted in the warm yellowish tint, which contrasts with the colder colour applied with coloured pencil. The reflections on the creature's body were done in the same manner.

The signature was painted in with blue acrylic.

The foam in the very fore is a mix of masked-off light blue ground and an application of light blue coloured pencil. An airbrush was used to modify the different values, both along the way and at the very end to darken the foam where needed. Water at low pressure in an airbrush can be used to re-dampen an area to blend colours more easily when it's not possible to return to that area with a brush. Clean water sprayed over brushwork will soften and blend colours, but it's necessary to take a good deal of care with dosing the pressure. The airbrush also allows easy darkening of the corners of the picture, since airbrush applied over brushwork is far less cold and mechanical than airbrush work alone.

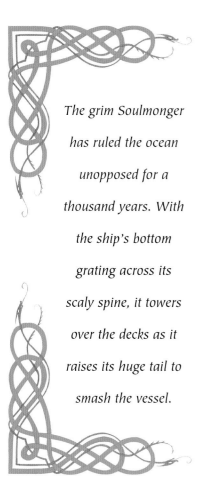

The grim Soulmonger has ruled the ocean unopposed for a thousand years. With the ship's bottom grating across its scaly spine, it towers over the decks as it raises its huge tail to smash the vessel.

DRAGONS OF EARTHSEA

I n Ursula K. Le Guin's world of Earthsea, the dragons were the firstborn, and they have lived long enough to gain profound wisdom. For a human to gain access to this knowledge, it is necessary to learn the Old Speech, the tongue in which wizards make spells, and which is innate to dragons. Communication of an even subtler kind – telepathy – enables the inhabitants of another fantasy world, Anne McCaffrey's planet Pern, to speak to dragons.

In many tales of heroic exploits, the dragon plays a role that is nothing but brute strength, huge size and gusts of fiery, venomous breath. Yet dragons are not simply cold beasts, foils for questing heroes to test their mettle. The ancient dragon was a creative force, and in the East dragons have always been respected as mysterious and powerful guardians of natural energies. The fate of dragons has recently improved though: writers of fantasy fiction have restored to the dragons of the West some of the wisdom and gravity that was lost when they began to do battle with saints.

The ancient Greek word *drakon*, for a huge serpent, is associated with another word that means 'I see clearly', acknowledging the dragon's perceptive powers. Both Greeks and Romans consulted the wisdom of dragons, protecting within temple precincts sacred serpents that spoke through the mouths of priestesses. The greatest of the oracles was at Delphi: here the god Apollo had killed and buried the serpent Python, an earth deity who guarded the centre of the world. The priestess of the oracle, known as the Pythia, dispensed arcane words of wisdom for a thousand years, in an atmosphere of ritual and trance that recalls shamanic practice.

Like shamans in their own world, Le Guin's dragonlords are set apart by their rare ability to conquer the difficulties of the ancient language and to be able to converse with dragons. The association with the heightened experience of a shaman runs through the story of the Norse dragon Fafnir, who prophesies as he dies and whose heart gives Sigurd the power of communication with other creatures. Tolkien took Fafnir's long conversation with Sigurd as a model for the talk between Bilbo Baggins and Smaug, who relishes riddles, lengthy titles and wordplay, as well as being susceptible to flattery.

TALKING TO A DRAGON

In Barbara Hambly's *Dragonsbane*, mageborn Jenny Waynest communicates directly with a sick dragon, perceiving his meaning in a swirl of sound and images in his silver eyes.

PERN DRAGONS
"Feline horses" would be the best words to describe Anne McCaffrey's dragons. Imagine creatures with the infinite grace and steel of the noblest horses and the supple, sensual, elegant diffidence of cats. Then add wings. You have the Dragons of Pern.

Anne McCaffrey
'PERN DRAGONS' WRITTEN AT DRAGONHOLD, WICKLOW

My dragons are not the reptilian kind with lots of scales and curls and writhing. While my Pernese dragons look more like horses than large snakes, they are not modelled after horses. Conversely, fire-lizards, the genetic base for Pernese dragons, are indeed cats. Very clever sympathetic fire-breathing cats.

Two things started me off on dragons: Andre Norton had once told me she thought dragons had a bad press in the West. I could agree with that. And John W. Campbell said you had to have a reason for putting alien beasts in a book: they had to fit a niche in that ecology.

Okay ... if I wanted to 'do' dragons why would they be needed? Dragons fly because they have wings. They can breathe fire because they have two stomachs like cows and digest a phosphene-bearing rock, which they chew (which is why they have a strong horse-type jaw) and when phosphene gas hits oxygen, it ignites.

You wouldn't want to have large creatures (2,530 feet long including tail) just whizzing about without some sort of control. So special people become dragon riders, impressing the hatchling at birth ... you, the rider, always have a friend who understands you completely. Dragons' tongues aren't made for speech so you resort to telepathy. So dragons are under control. Why does Pern need an airborne strike force?

Okay, there is an erratic planet in its solar system and its course takes it near Pern about every 250 years and drops a spore, which is hostile to everything vegetable or animal on the surface. So you need to destroy it above ground, which points to an aerial, flame-capable deterrent. Dragons and their special riders.

The dragons' blood is based on copper, rather than iron as ours is. So they are gold, bronze, brown, blue and green – colours that copper can have. They don't have scales, they have a hide like thick suede, and they smell cinnamony.

One can't illustrate such details but they go with thinking very hard about Pernese dragons so my readers can actually visualize them. Michael Whelan who got the cover contract from Ballantine, knew a lot more about saurian/reptilian critters. John has a different research base, but his Pern dragons are every bit a distinct species and for his versatility he is to be highly recommended for his attention to craft, detail and verisimilitude. He thinks about what dragons are and reproduces some fine specimens.

SKETCHING THE DRAGONS

Marine iguanas played a huge role in painting the dragons of Earthsea. I have no logical explanation for why any one creature somehow seems to be made of the 'right stuff' to serve as a model. It is far more the surreal juxtaposition of such strange creatures with their volcanic land- and seascape that served as inspiration, rather than any purely anatomical information: the idea of a fully mineral world, jutting from the depths of the ocean, peopled shoulder-to-shoulder with anthracite creatures of malevolence and power that are practically living rock. Reducing the various schemes – colour, composition, texture – to a very few elements increases the otherworldliness of a realm where any human venture becomes all the more unlikely and perilous.

DRAGON HEAD
Scales on reptiles are fascinating things: there's so much more to them than just a latticework of criss-crossed lines. They vary hugely in size and shape, can sport lumps, spines or fins, overlap or abut, and of course are never all quite the same colour.

EARTHSEA DRAGONS

Rather than copy specific details or body structure from
marine iguanas, it is their proximity to the sea that
whets my imagination. While I did keep their pebbly
hides and backs full of spines, the main ingredient
in the sketch is intent. Their attention is focused
on the horizon; something is approaching the
shores of their kingdom. Nevertheless, they
don't seem overly concerned – it's almost
as though they are listening to music.

The young wizard Ged sails stoically towards his encounter with the nine dragons on the isle of Pendor. The dragons of Earthsea have sharp hearing and keen sight, and they are alert to his approach. He is risking everything on his one chance to bind the Old Dragon to his will.

ICEFYRE AND THE STONE DRAGON

 he opposite of a fire-breathing dragon is a dragon of ice or frost. But is it any less deadly? It sparks and burns as dangerously and unpredictably as its fiery counterpart, or else it is frozen into immobility, but always with the potential to melt its cold prison and explode in billows of angry flame.

STONE DRAGON COVER VIGNETTE
Not very much can be done in a tiny vignette – despite getting carried away with a sketch half a yard square for a vignette that will be printed the size of a modest postage stamp. Images of this nature are like shorthand, hopefully to be revisited in the future with more latitude to paint.

Unlike Tolkein's cold-drake – a dragon that lacks fiery breath, perhaps of a dwindling and more ancient race than his mighty fire-drakes – an ice dragon would be capable of burning and destroying with cold, just as ice burns the skin if you touch it. Or it could be a dragon of air and fire, like Robin Hobb's great black dragon Icefyre who, according to legend, has been locked for millennia deep under the ice of the frozen island Aslevjal, waiting, pent like a coiled spring.

It's said that Chinese dragons fear fire, despite their fiery breath, because dragon fire and earthly fire are opposites: confronting a dragon with fire will extinguish its flames, whereas when dragon fire meets water it burns more fiercely. The idea of the ice dragon embraces a similar paradox: it is an elemental being of fire and air, yet it inhabits a world of water frozen and stonelike. The dragons of alchemy were mercurial and contradictory: they were the assimilation

of all opposites – lightness and dark, heat and cold – and they generated an energy that if harnessed could achieve transmutation. Dragons like Icefyre have the power to change the world, but not for the sake of good. They shake off any harness, their energy is purely explosive. Their power has nothing of the beneficial, but it is more akin to tectonics – a slowly building ire that will suddenly slip free and leave destruction and irreversible change in its wake. This violent opposition of transmutation in harmony to transfiguration through force underlies the entire body of Robin Hobb's work.

Obviously, none of this can be captured explicitly in one image – and leave room for the title and author's name to boot – but paramount to the conflict is the attitude of the combatants: one seeking headlong only destruction, the other seeking reconciliation, even in conflict.

ICE DRAGON

An image done to plug
a hole in a book layout,
but never used. For ages
I had, in the back of my
mind and the bottom of a
drawer, a lovely photo of
a rather rotund toad and
in another drawer, a photo
of a glacier. Suddenly the
two just seemed right for
each other.

Robin Hobb
CHOOSING TO BELIEVE IN DRAGONS

I choose to believe in dragons.

The dragons I believe in are the dragons of old, rather than the cuddly, pastel creatures of children's fare today. My dragons are arrogant and cunning, coldly calculating in their intelligence, cruel and ruthless to their enemies. In some tales, they share the human predilection for greed, amassing worldly goods far beyond their ability to consume or enjoy them. In Japan and China, they have a reputation for wisdom and sound judgment. In short, they are as varied as humans, and our equals in their drive to survive at all costs.

Yet the similarities my dragons share with their human counterparts can present a challenge to this writer as well as to the artist who depicts my draconian characters. In print or in paint, to be effective a dragon must remain a dragon and not a large, scaled human with wings. One reason to use a dragon as a character rather than as a natural disaster is to present something that is completely foreign to human values, intellect and emotions. I strive to depict the dragon as alien and 'other' than human. It's not easy. Can a dragon be written so that he has personality without humanity? Can a battle between dragons be painted in such a way that the viewer sees seasoned warriors in combat rather than animals fighting?

Over the years (more than a decade now) I have discovered that I can trust John to sift the words on the page and assemble the vision from my mind. Our contact has been more than correspondence. I send him words and he replies with pencil strokes and daubs of paint. Yet I always feel we are talking about the same thing. I've entrusted some of my dearest friends to him, friends of all species, and seen them transformed into flesh.

This correspondence has not been without surprises for me. Every time I look at the cover art for Assassin's

Quest, a book that features very unusual dragons, I see new details and discover nuances I've overlooked. When this happens, I often wonder, 'Did I write that? Or did John find it in the spaces between the lines?' The lovely part is that I feel John's cover art in general (not just his dragons) often enlarges the window I've opened into a world. I've never felt that any of his depictions limited the reader's view of the story. (Or the writer's, for that matter! On one occasion, a detail in his art – the twining of a vine around a sword blade – inspired part of a scene toward the end of the book it illustrated.) Rather, his illustrations have always gone beyond the edges of the text, as if a camera had been dollied back to show the larger picture. Certainly his dragons for the cover of Fool's Fate exemplify the old saying, 'A picture is worth 10,000 words.' Muscles straining, they are obviously creatures of air doomed to share a common enemy in gravity, yet willing to risk that end in their competition to be the sole survivor of the battle. There are details in that painting I don't recall writing, but obviously they belong there: the barbed wings and tails, the multitude of bared teeth, the heaving ribs. Pondering that picture, it becomes obvious to me that John Howe not only believes in dragons; he believes in the same ones that I do. I have absolutely no reservations in trusting him to depict them well.

I've long felt that humanity might benefit if we had to share this earth with a race of beings that were just as haughty and thoughtless about the world as we are. Dragons, real or fictional, might provide the perfect mirror to reveal us to ourselves. And if I can choose to believe in dragons that sometimes, despite all their flaws, reveal themselves as creatures both magnificent and noble, well, then, perhaps I can choose to believe that of humanity as well. And trust John to be able to reveal that in his paintings.

A SLEEPING DRAGON

Entombed in the translucent depths of a glacier, the Dragon Icefyre sleeps, awaiting the day at the end of days, when he must awaken for the battle that will decide the fate of the world.

ASSASSIN'S QUEST

The scene in Robin Hobb's book that stuck in my mind (unusually for me, since it's usually scenes of action and tension that catch my eye) was the one where the company of wanderers comes upon a forest clearing filled with statues – once-living creatures that have been turned to stone. (Sometimes, even in a high fantasy, the most mundane of scenes is the most striking, since you can *almost* imagine it happening to you.) I think I would approach the image very differently now, but at the time, this picture formed complete in my head on the spot.

I've always loved ivy on stone, and never miss an opportunity to photograph it. I have a huge collection of images of ivy-covered monuments residing in a drawer of their own: 'Brambles, Ivy & Leaves'.

The merging of the dragon's tail into the moss-covered ground is important – not only because it makes sense visually, but edges and borders in nature are rarely clear-cut frontiers.

I wish I could revisit this scene and do the characters properly, with their costumes, faces and personalities, but often, an illustration of this kind only serves to whet an appetite that cannot be satisfied.

ICEFYRE AND THE STONE DRAGON

PAINTING THE DRAGON

During his long imprisonment, it is as if the burning hate in Icefyre's heart has extruded to form ragged spines and vicious claws. I was quite pleased with the idea of his leading wing 'finger' becoming a sort of dagger, as if the joints had welded and it had grown sharp bone edges. His spine has arched back and his withers angle forward in a line no longer smooth and sinuous, but harsh and broken. His tail is contorted like a bramble, the leathery wings so shrunken that he can perhaps barely fly. Naturally, I made all this up, as it's not really specified in Robin Hobb's text, which contains references far more precious than simple physical details.

I thought I could get away with a brown dragon on black, but when the book was published Icefyre had turned a rather disconcerting (and patently much more visible) red. The book cover has since been republished elsewhere without any such 'improvements'.

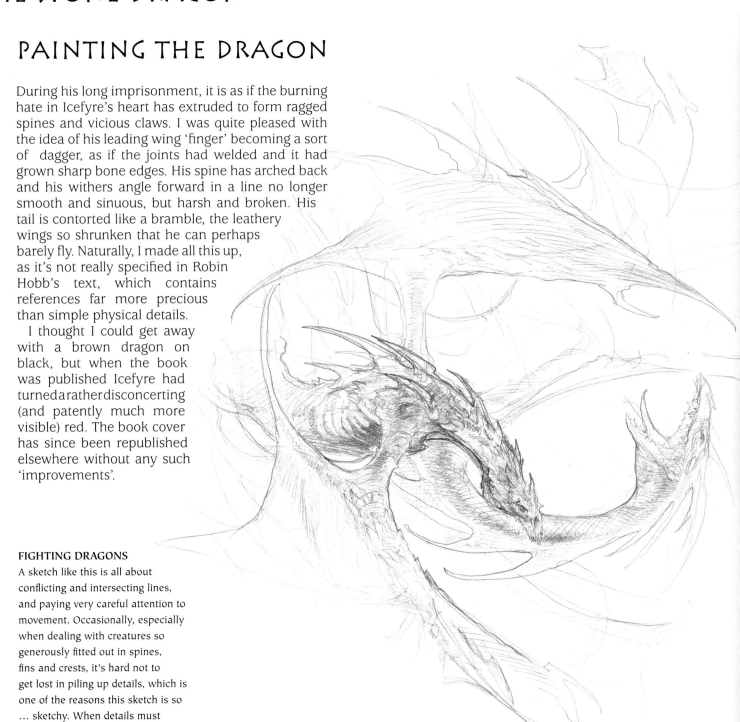

FIGHTING DRAGONS
A sketch like this is all about conflicting and intersecting lines, and paying very careful attention to movement. Occasionally, especially when dealing with creatures so generously fitted out in spines, fins and crests, it's hard not to get lost in piling up details, which is one of the reasons this sketch is so … sketchy. When details must be explored, they can be done on a different sketch entirely.

Icefyre is a
desiccated and
hateful creature
who has long
lain in wait,
encased in his icy
sarcophagus, for
his final struggle
with the Stone
Dragon.

SMAUG THE GOLDEN

Smaug is a dragon of splendour, with reddish-gold scales and wings and a jewel-encrusted breast. He is the last of the great fire-breathing dragons of Tolkien's Middle-earth, and smouldering in his lair under the Lonely Mountain he gloats over a great hoard of dwarvish and elven treasure. He is Smaug the Magnificent, he is ancient, he is clever...and he is conceited.

SMAUG

Another sketch that really *needs* to be done as a colour piece. With the moonlight falling across Smaug and the golden glow of the dragon and the glinting treasure, the whole fading into the murky depths of the hall, it would be a study in contrasts and reflected light. The columns are just blocked in to show their positions. The design itself will require a few more sketches – a brief foray into dwarven design.

Smaug has the super-sharp senses typical of dragonkind: he can smell intruders, keep watch with half an eye even while he sleeps, and exert a hypnotic power with his gaze. His careful guarding of his treasure, and his fury when he discovers that a single item – a cup – has been stolen from it, are borrowed directly from the story of Beowulf, which Tolkien acknowledged as one of his most important sources. Another was the legend of Sigurd and Fafnir, which the young Tolkien had discovered in Andrew Lang's 1890 collection, *The Red Fairy Book*: as a child he thought it the best story he had ever read. He modelled Bilbo's riddling conversation with Smaug on Fafnir's long dialogue with Sigurd, establishing that 'the way to talk to dragons' is by catching them up in the fascination of wordplay, half-truths, flattery and boasts. Smaug's boasting and vanity will prove to be his downfall, as Bilbo's flattery persuades him to show off his diamond waistcoat – and the bare and vulnerable patch of skin that will be found by Bard's arrow.

Smaug is one of only four named dragons in Middle-earth, though Tolkien described many others emerging from the fortress of Angband to destroy the enemies of the dark lord Morgoth. The oldest is the deceitful and cunning Glaurung, called the father of dragons, who is the first of the Urolóki, or fire-drakes, and is wingless. Ancalagon the Black is a winged fire-drake, and the largest dragon of Middle-earth; he leads a fleet of dragons to drive back the host of the Valar. Of Scatha the long-worm little is known, except that after his death disputes over his hoard provoke feuding among the dwarves. The fire-breathing dragons destroy four of the Dwarven Rings, but their heat is not enough to melt the One Ring.

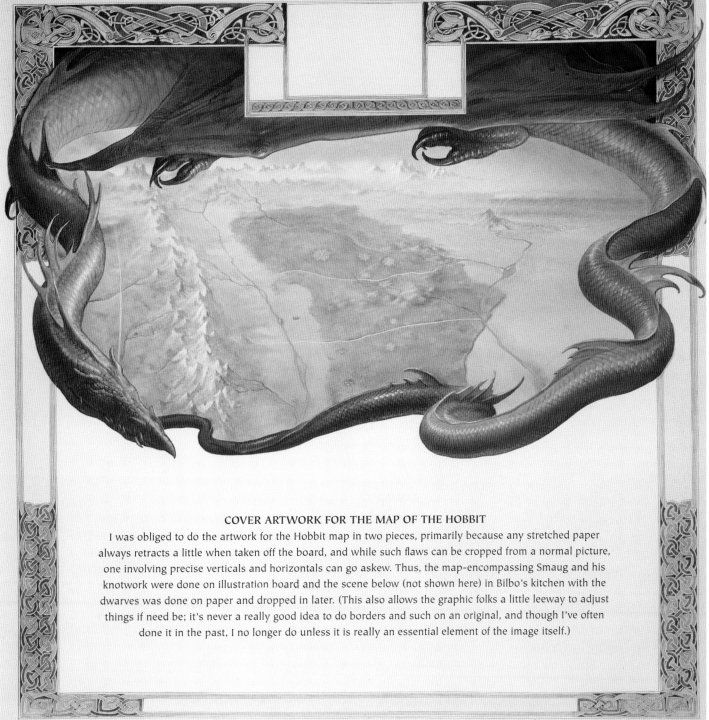

COVER ARTWORK FOR THE MAP OF THE HOBBIT

I was obliged to do the artwork for the Hobbit map in two pieces, primarily because any stretched paper always retracts a little when taken off the board, and while such flaws can be cropped from a normal picture, one involving precise verticals and horizontals can go askew. Thus, the map-encompassing Smaug and his knotwork were done on illustration board and the scene below (not shown here) in Bilbo's kitchen with the dwarves was done on paper and dropped in later. (This also allows the graphic folks a little leeway to adjust things if need be; it's never a really good idea to do borders and such on an original, and though I've often done it in the past, I no longer do unless it is really an essential element of the image itself.)

SMAUG THE GOLDEN

The dragon's hoard

All the dragons of Middle-earth share a burning greed for treasure, especially gold, and in *The Hobbit* a clear distinction is expressed between a love of craftsmanship and beauty, exemplified by the dwarves, and the blind greed of a hoarder who can neither use nor truly appreciate his possessions.

The association of dragons and gold is an ancient one, and in dragon lore there is more to the idea of the hoard than greed alone. Nagas and Chinese dragons also love treasure and preside over sumptuous palaces of gold and pearls. The dragon sleeping on his underground hoard of precious metal and gems is the serpent as an earth spirit, with access to the earth's mineral wealth.

Artemidorus, writing on the interpretation of dreams in the second century BC, theorized that dreaming of dragons signified imminent wealth and fruitfulness, and it was a dragon, Ladon, who watched over the golden apples of immortality growing in the mythical garden of the Hesperides.

In Norse mythology the hoard is usually associated with a burial, and the dragon keeps watch over treasure piled under a barrow, so he is the guardian of the grave as well as the treasure, connecting him with death and the afterlife. Dragons are thus guardians both of the tragic symbol of mortality – the yearning for eternal wealth despite the brevity of life, and the one gift that all inherit – death and eternity.

FEAR! FIRE! FOES!

This is a picture I don't care for very much, but it illustrates the pitfalls awaiting the overconfident. Intent on making a flawless blue sky and eager to paint the mountain lit by the last rays of the sun, I neglected to actually draw Smaug properly before masking him off. It was only when the tape had been peeled away and the (flawless) sky completed that I realized his neck was all wrong. Too late, I'd let the background lock me into an insufficiently thought-out foreground. I tried in vain to fix it, and ever since have had a burning desire to get back to Mount Doom and do the painting over again.

LEFT: SMAUG

Another version of Smaug, which I feel has a very 'classical' look. I like to imagine Tolkien saw him as quite a traditional dragon, and his own depictions do show a long and slender silhouette.

BILBO THE BURGLAR

This pencil drawing was part of a book of short essays by fantasy authors about their encounters with Tolkien's Middle-earth. How to depict an invisible Bilbo was an issue that Tolkien himself struggled with in his own illustrations, placing his Hobbit in a sort of magical cloud. I thought it made sense just to leave him out and play with shadows and contrasts.

PAINTING THE DRAGON

Smaug is simultaneously a storybook dragon and a deadly menace. *The Hobbit* lies between two worlds, the grown-up, mythological world of the (later) *The Lord of the Rings*, and a suspenseful bedtime story for small children. In a way, Smaug symbolizes the subtext of fairy tale – outwardly sweet and ultimately fierce when looked at more closely. A little convoluted, I admit, but it was very much in my mind while I was trying to bend his pliable neck in such a way that his chin could be posed on his crossed forefeet. I wanted him to be attractive and colourful, but not one-dimensional. He is Smaug the Golden, glorious and ridiculously vain, but still capable of great fury and destruction.

If I had to choose a few of my pictures to rescue from a fire or a sinking ship, this would likely be one of them. It is the very first cover for a Tolkien novel I did, in 1990. To draw the golden hoard, I gathered up a jar full of various European coins – the kind that, before the Euro, you brought back by the pocketful from any trip – and piled them on my table under the desk lamp, in order to try to figure out their particular way of reflecting light. The wisps of smoke arising from Smaug's nostrils were erased with a hard eraser where they are lit warmly, and added in coloured pencil farther up, where they are blue-grey.

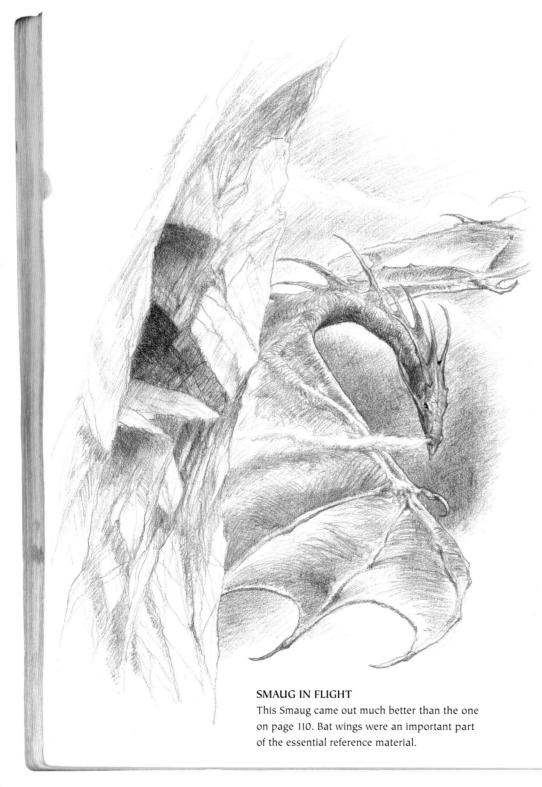

SMAUG IN FLIGHT
This Smaug came out much better than the one on page 110. Bat wings were an important part of the essential reference material.

Glowing red-gold
in his lair deep
within the Lonely
Mountain, Smaug
lies smokily
a-slumber on his
heap of stolen
treasure.

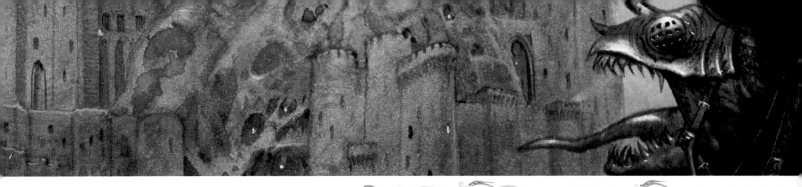

THE FELL BEASTS

I can already hear voices exclaiming 'But fell beasts aren't dragons!' The terrible winged monsters on which the Nazgûl ride into battle are not, true enough, dragons, but they share many of the physical characteristics. Also, they exemplify Tolkien's genius – a paucity of descriptive elements allowing an illustrator's imagination the freedom to roam. (I was going to write 'It's my book so I can put in what I like!' but the editor said it wouldn't make the right impression.)

EOWYN KILLS THE FELL BEAST
Eowyn's unequal combat against the Witch-king is born of the heroism of desperation, but to convey the disproportion of force every 'traditional' method – looming Nazgûl/small human, highlighting hero, cluttered battlefield – seemed inadequate. Instead, the sense of imbalance and conflict derives from the pose of the protagonists. Eowyn is in the eye of a storm, both engulfing her and recoiling from her. Both are locked into a dance of death, suspended for a split second on fate's fulcrum.

The creatures are not given a name, the lack of definition only adding to their aura of terror. Tolkien's strongest descriptions of creatures, people or places dwell on the sentiments they inspire rather than simple physical descriptions, allowing each reader to create a personal pantheon of horror or beauty. (Tolkien tells us of Elves through the eyes and words of Sam, whose hesitant – and to him inadequate – description is worth a hundred pages of meticulous detail.) Tolkien qualifies the Nazgûl's winged steeds with the archaic adjective 'fell', meaning fierce, cruel and sinister (and, in Scots, pungent, which is also appropriate to these stinking beasts).

The nine Nazgûl, or Ringwraiths, move in an aura of terror that affects all creatures that come near them, and their venomous breath fills their victims with despair. When they first appear in *The Lord of the Rings* they are mounted on black horses, specially bred and trained

The Nazgûl Lord Attacks

FROM J. R. R. TOLKIEN'S THE RETURN OF THE KING, CHAPTER 6

But lo! Suddenly in the midst of the glory of the king his golden shield was dimmed. The new morning was blotted from the sky. Dark fell about him. Horses reared and screamed. Men cast from the saddle lay grovelling on the ground.

'To me! To me!' cried Theoden. 'Up Eorlingas! Fear no darkness!' But Snowmane wild with terror stood up on high, fighting with the air, and then with a great scream he crashed upon his side: a black dart had pierced him. The king fell beneath him.

The great shadow descended like a falling cloud. And behold! it was a winged creature: if bird, then greater than all other birds, and it was naked, and neither quill nor feather did it bear, and its vast pinions were as webs of hide between horned fingers; and it stank. A creature of an older world maybe it was, whose kind, lingering in forgotten mountains cold beneath the Moon, outstayed their day, and in hideous eyrie bred this last untimely brood, apt to evil. And the Dark Lord took it, and nursed it with fell meats, until it grew beyond the measure of all other things that fly; and he gave it to his servant to be his steed. Down, down it came, and then, folding its fingered webs, it gave a croaking cry, and settled upon the body of Snowmane, digging in its claws, stooping its long naked neck.

Upon it sat a shape, black-mantled, huge and threatening. A crown of steel he bore, but between rim and robe naught was there to see, save only a deadly gleam of eyes: the Lord of the Nazgûl. To the air he had returned, summoning his steed ere the darkness failed, and now he was come again, bringing ruin, turning hope to despair, and victory to death. A great black mace he wielded.

THE FELL BEASTS

in Mordor to endure the terror of their riders. The horses are drowned when Elrond and Gandalf create a flood in the river Bruinen, and the Ringwraiths are forced to return to Mordor. They re-emerge in a new, even more terrifying guise on the fell beasts.

Compared with the dragons of Middle-earth, such as the guileful Glaurung and the vainglorious Smaug, the fell beasts are primitive creatures with no independence of will or deed. Evoking pterosaurs, though much larger, their hide wings, stretched between 'horned fingers', are like those of bats. Tolkien himself admitted he 'did not intend the steed of the Witch-king to be what is now called a "pterodactyl", although the creature is 'obviously ... pterodactylic and owes much' to the 'new ... mythology of the "Prehistoric", possibly being 'a last survivor of older geological eras.'[2]

NAZGÛL

I imagined that the Nazgûl, once airborne, might be dressed in their full harness from head to toe, complete with lance and shield if need be.

BARAD-DÛR

Mordor is not just a blighted landscape, it is an extension of Sauron's gangrened soul. Barad-dûr's foundations are anchored in his folly, his wrath embodied in battlement piled on battlement, his power the mortar that holds stone to stone. The land itself is his image. The image began fairly simply: 'It would be great to capture the vertiginous impossible nature of Barad-dûr, but then a shot at the Red Eye wouldn't hurt, and while the background is still damp, how about squeezing in Mount Doom? Oh yes, and a Nazgûl or two would be nice while you're at it. And don't forget, lots of smoke, didn't I mention that the Ring had just fallen into the crack of Doom?' Directors...

The air itself is poisoned by Sauron's breath, and the sky is torn by the cries of his servants.

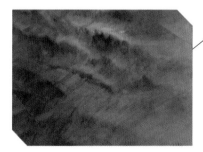

The parched plain of Gorgoroth appears as if a storm-wracked sea suddenly solidified into stone, pitted and decayed but honed razor-sharp by the very negation of life the Dark Lord represents.

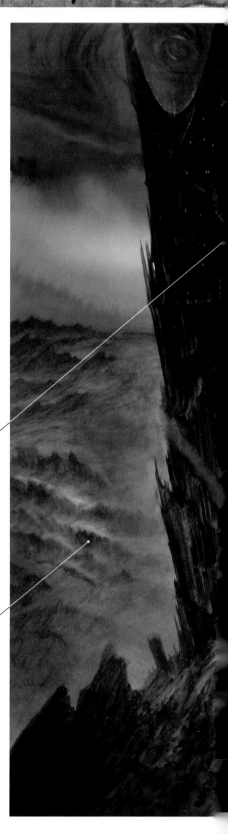

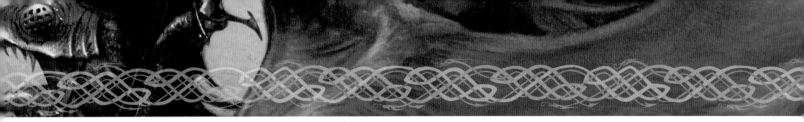

THE FELL BEASTS

SKETCHING THE FELL BEAST

I drew my very first depiction of a Nazgûl when I was about 16, happily going through the books picking out the scenes with the greatest potential for action and mayhem. Naturally Theoden's fateful encounter with the Witch-king was well up on my list and I painted a huge green pterodactyl with a rider that resembled Frank Frazetta's Death Dealer (the top half anyway, I hid his legs behind those handy fell wings). Poor Theoden was toppling backwards off a rearing Snowmane, I suppose largely in dismay because the picture was just so awful. Naturally, I wasn't going to stop at green pterosaurs, and the next fell beast, drawn a few years later, was based on a very creepy mummified fish in the Natural History Museum of Nancy, in France. (I still have the photo I took and the painting – unfinished – somewhere.) The next return of the fell beast took place in 1990, for the 1991 Tolkien Calendar, with the creature perched on a crag before the Dark Tower.

Clouds of soot and ash hang low over the plain, and dark creatures scream and wheel in the sky, swooping on bat-like wings: all who hear them cower.

THE WITCH-KING
After vainly trying to draw the Witch-king on his high saddle atop the fell beast, I realized that I was erroneously trying to depict him as a sort of extension of the movement of the creature, rather than allowing him to create his own centre of gravity. Sometimes, an eraser is your best friend...

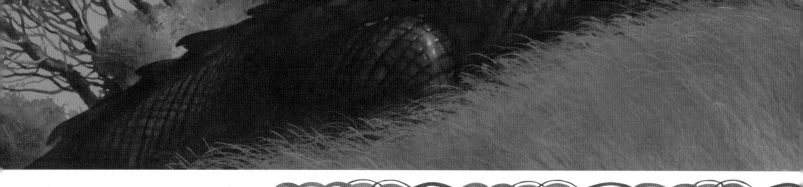

GLAURUNG

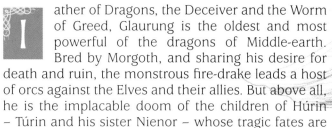

Father of Dragons, the Deceiver and the Worm of Greed, Glaurung is the oldest and most powerful of the dragons of Middle-earth. Bred by Morgoth, and sharing his desire for death and ruin, the monstrous fire-drake leads a host of orcs against the Elves and their allies. But above all, he is the implacable doom of the children of Húrin – Túrin and his sister Nienor – whose tragic fates are intertwined with Glaurung's own end.

The once-fair halls of ruined Nargothrond are Glaurung's lair. There, with all the insatiable greed of his kind, he sprawls atop a great hoard of treasure. Glaurung has the power of an enchanter: the evil glamour of his hypnotic gaze can bewilder his victims and bring false thoughts unbidden to their minds. He persuades Túrin to desert the battlefield, wrongly believing his mother and sister to be in danger. Túrin hastens homeward, abandoning the Elf Finduilas, who loves him, to her fate at the hand of the orcs who have captured her. Then Glaurung uses his fell power to empty Nienor's mind so that when she meets Túrin they do not know each other. Unaware that they are brother and sister, they fall in love and are married.

When Glaurung attacks the men of Haleth in the forest of Brethil, Túrin waits until the great wyrm throws his huge body across the ravine of Cabed-en-Aras of the River Taeglin, and, climbing from below, he stabs Glaurung in the belly with his black sword. Unconscious, overcome by the dragon's venomous blood that has spilt on him, Túrin is unaware of Nienor's arrival. Glaurung, even as he is dying, delivers the stroke that will seal her doom: he lifts the spell-veil from Nienor's eyes and she remembers her true name. Horrified at her incestuous union, she throws herself into the ravine.

Glaurung's great corpse has gone cold, but Túrin's doom is not yet run. Brandir, ruler of Haleth, has witnessed Nienor's death, but Túrin refuses to believe him and slays him in anger. When he learns the truth, he falls in despair on the sword he used to kill Glaurung, and he is buried along with its broken shards.

SKETCH FOR THE KILLING OF GLAURUNG
A quick sketch of the scene, with Túrin clinging to the cliff and driving Gurthang straight up into Glaurung's belly. Though much more satisfying graphically, it did not allow a portrayal of the dragon, so the option opposite was chosen. Proof that an interesting idea is never lost, only delayed, I later recycled it as a pencil drawing for the Map of Beleriand.

THE KILLING OF GLAURUNG

This image is not really about Glaurung at all, it's all about elements – water, earth and fire. Technically, it began with one of those volatile splashes of incompatible colours – yellow and vermillion on grey and blue. The dark body of Glaurung is almost part of the rock, and the water was masked by spattering latex from a toothbrush over an already lightly coloured and textured ground. Contrary to my habits at the time, I was sensible enough *not* to mask Túrin Turambar, instead relying on the dark rock around him, which was filled in once he was painted. It's worthwhile always to ask the question, 'Do I *really* need to mask an element off?' before making it a systematic practice.

GLAURUNG

SKETCHING THE DRAGON

A decade or so ago I was working on illustrations for a collectable card game, and 'Dragon's Curse' – the moment of Túrin's death – came around. I might have known that, with such a title, the commission was doomed, and indeed it looks as if Glaurung's curse didn't stop with Húrin's children.

I happily submitted a sketch of Túrin Turambar in a three-quarters back view, fallen to his knees with his sword sticking up between his shoulder blades, which I thought would work very well. His hands had fallen open on his knees, and his hair hung down from his bowed head; he was finally at peace.

The editor turned it down, and asked for the moment before he impales himself.

So, new sketch.

Three-quarter front view this time, but with the whole body suspended just on the tip of the blade, poised to drop himself on to it, once again with his head hanging down, hair obscuring the face. I was still pleased enough, with the face hidden by his hair, the hands gripping the blade, the awkward turned-in feet, everything poised on that fatal instant.

Unfortunately for me…

His back was 'too rounded', I was told, poor Túrin looked 'depressed'. (I wouldn't have been at all jolly at throwing myself on my sword, but fair enough.) He needed a good straightening up; the editor 'needed to see his face'. He had to look 'more angry'.

Likely, I did another sketch (since lost, if I did indeed do one), which must have been approved. Actually doing the colour final was a very unhappy moment. The sword is boring (part of the problem in working on large series with other illustrators is the obligation to conform to existing – and often boring – design); the pose is awful; Túrin's grimacing face is painful to contemplate; even Glaurung looks faintly embarrassed at being involved, even though he is dead.

The colour piece, though I'm certainly guilty of doing it, is the product of so many hands it doesn't feel as if it's really mine. (That's why it's not in this book.)

This is a scene I hope one day to do – without interference – and finally do it justice.

NIENOR AND GLAURUNG

I wanted to place the fatal encounter between Nienor and Glaurung in a setting that would be idyllic were it not for the drama unfolding. (I've always loved windy hills or seaside cliffs, with the trees sculpted by the wind.) There was really little point in doing a detailed sketch of Nienor's face (I never get sketches the way I want anyway, it's only when I get a brush instead of a pencil that I can happily explore faces) since she ended up being quite small in the painting. But it did help in determining her attitude – a mix of courage and dread.

Another view (left) shows the same scene, perhaps a minute or two later. The dragon is awful – he looks rather chubby and mischievous instead of baleful and deadly, but that is the kind of thing one fixes properly when the original painting is under way.

By raising a noisome cloud of vapour the dragon Glaurung
scatters Nienor's companions and ambushes her alone on
the Spyhill. There he induces her to stare into his eyes and
empties her mind, even stealing her name.

A FAREWELL TO DRAGONS
(THOUGH IT'S REALLY JUST AN AU REVOIR)

We seem to take fantasy very much for granted. Of course, it no longer carries the same meaning as it did in the days of Ovid, Chrétien de Troyes or the Brothers Grimm, and that metamorphosis has been permanent, but while the cast and their quests are continually renewed and the stage often reset, the themes never change. In this unfolding, ever-changing but constant drama, dragons have always played a role. They are among the First. They are the imperfection gnawing at the universe in the oldest tales; they are the mirrors of our own human imperfection in the most modern fiction. In a way, they embody the parts of us we can never be rid of and which we can never fully realize.

Sárkánykígyó, ryu, wyvern, drac, cuélebre, y ddraig goch, naga, imoogi, lindworm, azhdah and hundreds more, from all corners of the world – the draconic family tree has more branches than Yggdrasil, and roots that go as deep. Those with names are legion: Nidhoggr, Melusine, Apep, Ouroboros or Tiamat. Their modern cousins – Ancalagon, Temeraire, Smaug, Vivacia, Ramoth or Glaurung – are likely equal in number and certainly their match in girth and guile.

The humans who tangle with them are no slouches either, be they saints of all sorts, helmed heroes of myth or farmers from Ham. Nor is any period in human history neglected in their stories: from the original Chaos to Midgard and Middle-earth, and on to the speculative realms of science fiction, there's always likely to be a dragon lurking.

Isn't that really a rather extraordinary curriculum vitae for creatures that don't exist?

And why yet another book on them? The answers are several. They embody concepts of considerable importance and they are clothed in scales. Their origins are inextricably interwoven with our psyche and they breathe fire. They are Freudian and, better still, eminently Jungian, and they spread vast wings over the sky. Few creatures combine such depth of meaning with such a rich palette for an illustrator.

So that's why. In a nutshell, not only are they fun to draw, they're more than just pretty faces. Like so many other things that exist only in our imaginations, they are so deep and complex that one drawing – or a thousand – will never be enough to get to know them properly.

ABOUT THE AUTHOR

JOHN HOWE was born in Vancouver in 1957 and grew up in British Columbia. He can't remember ever not drawing and John's talents and passion for the arts became evident at a young age; he then went on to study at the Ecole des Arts Décoratifs de Strasbourg. A gifted painter, illustrator and writer of children's books, John has been highly acclaimed for his work on J.R.R. Tolkien's books and associated merchandise over the last two decades. In recent years, John and fellow Tolkien illustrator Alan Lee, has mesmerized audiences across the globe with their award-winning work as Conceptual Designers for Peter Jackson's *Lord of the Rings* film trilogy. John's work can frequently be seen in exhibitions throughout Europe, recently appearing at the prestigious Bibliothèque Nationale de Paris.

John's imaginative power is truly an inspiration. He is passionate about the need to construct fantasy on a foundation of authenticity, creating a world that is plausible and familiar in some way. His knowledge of the Medieval period is outstanding, and as a practitioner of living history, he extends his experience and knowledge of weapons, armour and fighting styles through re-enactments. This energy spills into his work – a distinct fusion of Medieval, Gothic and Art Noveau inspirations. And inextricably woven into John's fabric of detail, is his love of mythology and heroic tales. Combining serious craftsmanship and technical skill, vitality of communication and depth of dimensionality, John's art is as experimental as it is visual. John lives in Switzerland with wife Fataneh (also an illustrator) and son Dana.

To view John's portfolio visit www.john-howe.com

ACKNOWLEDGMENTS

Thanks first of all to Freya Dangerfield for believing this book could be done.

Thanks to Beverley Jollands for patiently hunting down so many great wyrms and cornering them in time to extract all their vital statistics.

To Anne McCaffrey and to Robin Hobb for their wise words, my most heartfelt thanks. They, and authors like them, have done much for a vanished species grandly in need of protection. They keep dragons alive in their words. They help us keep them alive in our minds.

Especial thanks to Guillermo del Toro, who provided much more than a simple foreword. I could not have hoped for finer words, which sum up those personal and universal yearnings that inhabit those for whom fantasy is an essential ingredient of reality.

Thanks to the anonymous engraver who so carefully incised 'Here Be Dragons' on the Lenox Globe in the early 1500s, thus expertly filling in a pesky blank spot and providing an apophthegm worthy of the most fervent of dragon-lovers and dragon-seekers since.

Thanks be for dragons.

Footnotes
[1] page 36 Paul Radin, *Primitive Man as Philosopher*, D. Appleton & Company, New York and London, 1927
[2] page 116 Humphrey Carpenter, ed. *The Letters of J. R. R. Tolkien*, Houghton Mifflin, Boston, 1981

INDEX

A
airbrushing 17, 26, 38, 93
alchemy 36–7, 102
amphisbaena 18
Ananta 10
Ancalagon 108, 126
Ancient Egypt 30–6, 84
anecdote, visual 16
Apep 30–5, 126
Apollo 96
Apsu 24
archetypes 36
architecture 14–15
Asgard 42
Assassin's Quest 104–5
Atar 48
Azi Dahaka 48

B
Babylonians 19, 24–9, 72, 84
Barad-Dûr 116–17, 119
Beowulf 48, 60–5, 67, 108
bestiaries 78

C
chaos 10, 24–7, 30, 36, 90, 126
Chinese tradition 10–11, 55, 102, 104, 110
Christianity 36, 72, 78
claws 75
cockatrice 19
composition 16–17
Conan 16–17
cosmic dragons 22–51
creation myths 10, 24–6, 28–9, 84
curses 66
curves 17
Cyrus 48

D
Daniel 48
Delphic oracle 96
design 16–17
detail 17, 75
dinosaurs 55
draconite 36
Dragon Hills 54–5
Drakhaoul 19
drawing stations 12–13

E
Ea 24
earth goddesses 48, 84
Earthsea 96–101
Eastern Europe 19
Elaine 80
elements 36, 121
elephants 78, 79
elves 18–19

Ethiopia 78, 79
evil 25, 30–5, 78, 84
eyes 12

F
Fafnir 66–71, 96, 108
fell beasts 114–19
fire 12, 48–51, 63–4
Fool's Fate 104
France 19

G
Galahad 80
Gaudi 14, 15
George, St 14, 15, 54, 72–7
Glaurung 108, 116, 120–5, 126
Grail 80
Greek myth 48, 84, 96, 110
Grendel 60–1

H
Hambly, Barbara 96
Hera 84
Heracles/Hercules 15, 18, 72
heroes 52–3, 60–87
highlights 82, 93
Hinduism 10, 36, 84
Hobb, Robin 56, 91, 102, 104–6
Hobbit, The 7, 108–13
horses 11, 74, 76–7
Hriedmar 66
Hydra 15, 18
Hymir 42

I
Icefyre 102–7
imperial dragons 10–11
inspiration 12, 14, 20, 44
Isolde 80

J
javelin snakes 78
Jömungandr 36, 42, 44
Jung, Carl 36

K
Kraken 90
Kur 25

L
Laidly Worm, The 66
Lamia 84
lampreys 45
Lancelot 78–83
landscapes 54–9
Le Guin, Ursula K. 96
Leviathan 90
life drawings 12, 20–1, 44, 86–7, 98
Lilith 84

lindworms 19
Liveship trilogy 91
Lord of the Rings trilogy 7, 114–19

M
Ma'at 30
McCaffrey, Anne 96, 97
maps 78, 79
Marduk 24, 26, 28–9, 72
Martha, St 72
Mayans 36
Melusine 84–7, 126
Merlin 55
mermaids 85, 86
Michael, St 14, 16, 72, 73
Middle Earth 7, 108–11, 114–19, 126
Midgard 42, 126
mountains 56–9

N
nagas serpents 10
narrative images 16
Nazgûl 114–19
Nidhoggr 42–7, 126
Nienor 120, 123, 125
Ninurta 25
Norns (Fates) 42
Norse myth 36, 42–7, 66–71, 96, 108, 110
Notre-Dame 14, 15

O
oceans 32–5, 58–9, 90–5
Odin 42, 66
Ouroboros 15, 18, 36–41, 126

P
Peluda 19
pens, fine quill 37
Pern dragons 96, 97
Perseus 72
Persian myth 11, 48
philosopher's stone 36
Pliny the Elder 78, 79
poster images 16
Python 96

R
Ragnarok 42, 44
Raymond of Poitou 85
Re 30–5
Regin 66, 71
renewal, symbols of 36, 40
reptiles 12, 20, 44, 98
Roman myth 96
Rustem 11

S
Satan 72, 78
scales 45, 75, 82, 98

sea serpents 90–5
serpent-women 84–7
Set 30, 31
shape-shifters 66–8
signatures 93
Sigurd 66, 68–9, 71, 96, 108
skin 12
Smaug 7, 12, 48, 96, 108–13, 116, 126
smoke 12
snakes/serpents 10, 15, 18, 36–42, 44, 78, 84–7, 90–5, 126
solar barques 31, 32–5
stars 25–6, 28–9
stone dragons 14–15, 102–7
Sturlusson, Snorri 44
subconscious 9, 44
Sumerians 24–9
symbolism 10, 16, 24, 26–7, 36, 40, 90

T
Tarasque 19, 84
Thor 42, 44
Tiamat 24–9, 72, 126
Tolkien, J.R.R. 44, 60, 96, 102, 108–25
transformation 66–8
treasure 60, 108, 110, 112–13, 120
Tristan 80
Túrin 120–2
Typhoeus 48

U
Underworld 25, 30
Utgard 42

V
varieties of dragon 18–19
Vikings 42, 55, 60
volcanoes 48–51, 57–9
Vortigern 54–5
Vouivre 84
Vulcan 48

W
Welsh dragon 54–5
wings 18–19
woodlands 74–7
Worm's Head 55
wyrms 18
wyverns 19

Y
Yggdrasil 42–7

Z
Zeus 48, 84
Zoroastrianism 48

CREDITS

Alamy: 15 (l) / British Library Images Online: 54, 60 (r), 79 (l) / British Museum Images: 24, 72 (bl) / Corbis: 15 (tl, bl, blm, br), 66, 85 (tl) / © 2004 Electronic Arts Inc. All rights reserved. Reprinted with permission from Electronic Arts Inc.: cover, 21, 98, 110 (bl) / Getty Images: 25, 79 (r) / © John Howe. Reproduced courtesy of HarperCollins*Publishers*: 4–5, 48, 56 (tl), 88–89, 90–91 (t), 91 (br), 92–93 (t), 93, 94–95, 102, 102–103 (t), 104, 104 (m), 105 (t, m), 106 (t), 107, 108–109 (t), 109, 110–111 (t), 112 (t), 113, 114 (t, b), 116–117, 118 (t), 119, 120 (t), 121, 122–123 (t), 124–125 / © New Line Productions, Inc. All rights reserved. *The Lord of the Rings, The Fellowship of the Ring, The Two Towers*, and *The Return of the King*, and the names of the characters, events, items, and places therein, are trademarks of The Saul Zaentz Company d/b/a Tolkien Enterprises under licenses to New Line Productions, Inc.: 116, 117 / reprinted with permission from RACKHAM © 2008 RACKHAM: 18–19 (t) / first published © 2005 Sophisticated Games Ltd. From Beowulf Board Game by Reiner Knizia, art by John Howe: 52–53, 60–61 (t), 61, 62–63 (t), 63 (b), 64–65; from War of the Ring Board Game by di Meglio, Maggi and Nepitello, art by John Howe: 115 (t) / *Meditations on Middle-Earth* published by St. Martin's Press 2002, artwork © John Howe: 111, 112 / *Beowulf* published by Templar Publishing: 52–53, 60–61 (t), 61, 62–63 (t), 63 (b), 64–65, 126–127 / TopFoto: 15 (tr, brm), 36, 84; from 'The Ancient Art & Architecture collection Ltd': 85 (br); from 'City & County of Swansea': 55 / Werner Forman Archive: 30, 31 (tl, br), 42 (bl), 60 (bl).